VIRGO

24 AUGUST – 23 SEPTEMBER

First published in Great Britain 2011
by Mills & Boon, an imprint of Harlequin (UK) Limited,
Eton House, 18-24 Paradise Road, Richmond, Surrey TW9 1SR

Copyright © Dadhichi Toth 2011

ISBN: 978 0 263 89656 5

Design by Jo Yuen Graphic Design
Typeset by KDW DESIGNS

Harlequin (UK) policy is to use papers that are natural, renewable
and recyclable products and made from wood grown in sustainable
forests. The logging and manufacturing processes conform to the
legal environmental regulations of the country of origin.

Printed and bound in Spain
by Blackprint CPI, Barcelona

Dedicated to

The Light of Intuition

Sri V. Krishnaswamy—mentor and friend

With thanks to

Joram and Isaac

Special thanks to

Nyle Cruz for

initial creative layouts and ongoing support

ABOUT DADHICHI

Dadhichi is one of Australia's foremost astrologers and is frequently seen on television and in other media. He has the unique ability to draw from complex astrological theory to provide clear, easily understandable advice and insights for people who want to know what their futures may hold.

In the 26 years that Dadhichi has been practising astrology, face reading and other esoteric studies, he has conducted over 10,000 consultations. His clients include celebrities, political and diplomatic figures, and media and corporate identities from all over the world.

Dadhichi's unique blend of astrology and face reading helps people fulfil their true potential. His extensive experience practising Western astrology is complemented by his research into the theory and practice of Eastern forms of astrology.

Dadhichi has been a guest on many Australian television shows, and several of his political and worldwide forecasts have proved uncannily accurate. He appears regularly on Australian television networks and is a columnist for online and offline Australian publications.

His websites—www.dadhichi.com and www.facereader.com—attract hundreds of thousands of visitors each month, and offer a wide variety of features, helpful information and services.

MESSAGE FROM DADHICHI

Hello once again and welcome to your 2012 horoscope book!

Can you believe it's already 2012? Time flies by so quickly and now here we are in this fateful year, a time for which several religions of the world—including the Mayans from 3100BC—have predicted some extraordinary events that are supposedly going to affect us all!

Some people are worried there will be a physical cataclysm that will kill millions and millions. Some are of the opinion it is the end of the economic and social models we have lived by for thousands of years. Others seem to believe the Planet Nibiru will whiz by planet Earth and beam up the 144,000 Chosen Ones.

Whatever the opinion, it is an undeniable fact that we are experiencing some remarkable worldwide changes due to global warming (even though that remains a point of contention) and other societal shifts. Scientific knowledge continues to outrun our ability to keep up with it, and time appears to be moving faster and faster.

But my own research has categorically led me to repeat: 'Relax, everyone; it is *not* the end of the world!' There will most certainly be a backlash at some point by Mother Earth at the gross unconsciousness of many of us. There will be ravaging storms, earthquakes and other meteorological phenomena that will shake the Earth, hopefully waking up those of us still in a deep sleep, dreaming, or possibly even sleepwalking. It is time to open our eyes and take responsibility.

If there are any significant global changes I foresee, they are the emergence of wider self-government and the greater Aquarian qualities of the coming New Age. This period is the cusp or changeover between the Age of Pisces, the Fish, and the Age of Aquarius, the Dawn of Higher Mankind.

Astrology, and these small books I write about it, are for the sole purpose of shedding light on our higher selves, alerting us to the need to evolve, step up to the plate, and assume responsibility for our thoughts, words and deeds, individually and collectively. The processes of karma are ripe now as we see the Earth's changes shouting to us about our past mistakes as a civilisation.

I hope you gain some deeper insight into yourself through these writings. For the 2012 series I have extended the topics and focused more on relationships. It is only through having a clear perception of our responsibility towards others that we can live the principles of astrology and karma to reach our own self-actualisation, both as individuals and as a race.

I hope you see the light of truth within yourself and that these words will act as a pointer in your ongoing search.

All the best for 2012.

Your Astrologer,

www.dadhichi.com
dadhichitoth@gmail.com
Tel: +61 (0) 413 124 809

CONTENTS

✿ CONTENTS ✿

CONTENTS
CONTINUED

VIRGO
PROFILE

LIFE IS LIKE A GAME OF CARDS.
THE HAND THAT IS DEALT TO YOU
REPRESENTS DETERMINISM; THE
WAY YOU PLAY IT IS FREE WILL.

Jawaharlal Nehru

VIRGO SNAPSHOT

Key Life Phrase		I Serve
Zodiac Totem		The Virgin
Zodiac Symbol	♍	
Zodiac Facts		Sixth sign of the zodiac; common, barren, feminine and dry
Zodiac Element		Earth
Key Characteristics		Loving, susceptible, sympathetic, sensual, faithful, instinctive, charitable, over-reactive and moody
Compatible Star Signs		Taurus, Cancer, Scorpio, Capricorn
Mismatched Signs		Aries, Sagittarius, Aquarius and Pisces

Ruling Planet		Mercury
Love Planet	♥	Saturn
Finance Planet	💲	Venus
Speculation Planet		Saturn
Career Planets	👤	Mercury, Saturn and Uranus
Spiritual and Karmic Planets	✿	Venus and Saturn
Friendship Planet		Moon
Destiny Planet		Saturn
Famous Virgos	★★	Cameron Diaz, Keanu Reeves, Sean Connery, Pink, Salma Hayek, Adam Sandler, Hugh Grant, Jack Black, Paul Walker, Stephen King, Jason Alexander, Shania Twain, Chris Tucker, Jada Pinkett Smith, Shannon Elizabeth, Lance Armstrong, Beyoncé Knowles, Nicole Richie, Faith Hill and Rose McGowan

Lucky Numbers and Significant Years	5, 6, 8, 14, 15, 17, 23, 24, 26, 32, 33, 35, 41, 42, 44, 50, 51, 53, 60, 62, 68, 71, 77 and 80
Lucky Gems	Green jade, emerald, green quartz, diamond and white coral
Lucky Fragrances	Lavender, chamomile, verbena, patchouli, peppermint, rosemary, basil, black pepper and lemon
Affirmation/ Mantra	I am relaxed and deserve to be served as well as serve
Lucky Days	Wednesday, Friday and Saturday

VIRGO OVERVIEW

Virgo is naturally shy and modest. And what you see is what you get. Often people might mistrust you, thinking you're pretending to be something you're not. You have a tendency to be a little guarded, especially when first meeting people. You're not quick to reveal too much of yourself, which is what others may perceive as guardedness within you.

In general, you are a meticulous person, although let me say that I have met some Virgos who are meticulous in only a few areas of their lives. For example, you may be particularly tidy and organised in seven out of eight bedrooms in your house, allowing yourself the luxury of being completely untidy in one.

On the other hand, this meticulousness and organisational ability may, in some Virgos, relate only to their mental and psychological make-up. You have an extraordinary ability for facts and figures by compartmentalising different ideas in your own mind, but when it comes to reproducing this in your work and living environment, you sometimes fall short of the mark. But that's only in some cases. Virgo is, for the most part, a tidy and organised sign, which reflects the need for perfectionism at the heart of your personality.

While other people don't understand your reasoning at times, this doesn't bother you. You are committed to doing your best in whatever line of work you've chosen, to make sure the end results are in keeping with your high standards.

You are practical rather than idealistic, but always diligent in delivering what you promise. You need to be careful of this drive for perfection, of serving others and running yourself into the ground or, indeed, making yourself sick. There are times when your nervous system will take a battering because of your intense desire to please others and make good on your promises. You need to balance these extremes in your nature so that they don't affect you in the long term.

CRITICAL VIRGO!

You have an eye for detail and know what you want.
You are highly critical of others who don't do their
best. You want others to live up to your standards.

You are a clean person. Virgo is the sixth sign of the zodiac, ruled by Mercury, so being clean, looking after your health, and eating to keep up your wellbeing are all important in your life. In fact, you hate any sort of health hazard and, in the extreme, can become hypochondriacal, agonising over every ache and pain you feel

Virgo's Perfectionism

Your perfection drives you in many ways to live your life on the platforms of service and quality work, rather than on those of money, power, ego and fame.

Part of your life's lesson is learning how to manage your criticism of both yourself and others. There is wisdom in what you have to say, but at times the way you say it can challenge those in relationships with you.

You need to learn the lessons of discrimination and relaxation, and understand that the idea of perfection varies from individual to individual. If you can find this all-important balance in the way you see the world and live your life, you will be able to exist in better harmony with others.

VIRGO CUSPS

ARE YOU A CUSP BABY?

Being born on the changeover of two star signs means you have the qualities of both. Sometimes you don't know whether you're Arthur or Martha, as they say! Some of my clients can't quite figure out if they are indeed their own star sign, or the one before, or after. This is to be expected because being born on the borderline means you take on apects of both. The following outlines give an overview of the subtle effects of these cusp dates and how they affect your personality quite significantly.

Virgo–Leo Cusp

If you happen to be born during the period from the 21st to the 28th of August, you're born on the borderline or cusp of Leo, the fifth sign of the zodiac, and your own, the sixth sign. As such, you are ruled by both the Sun and the planet Mercury. This makes you a person of a sunny disposition with a strong intellectual leaning.

Being methodical, you're inclined to be a hard worker, but unlike the typical Virgo, you have no problem standing in the limelight and being the centre of attention, taking full credit for anything and everything you do.

UNIQUE INTUITION

*With a mixture of solar and Mercurial energies, you
have a unique intuition that serves you well. You
understand the people you come into contact with
through having amazingly subtle intellectual flashes,
which you usually trust.*

Unfortunately, if you're not recognised for what you do,
unlike the typical Virgo, you may start to feel inwardly
unfulfilled and frustrated. Over time, this will adversely
impact on your health, so you must find ways of bringing
this part of your nature out into the open, to not develop
grudges and become a closed-off person.

You have an unusual blend of extroverted and introverted
qualities, which puts you in the perfect position to
associate with all sorts of people. There are times when
others don't understand you, however, because you
swing between these two extremes of your personality.

Virgo–Libra Cusp

If you were born between the 14th and the 21st of
September, you fall in the area of the zodiac that is
jointly governed by two star signs: Virgo and Libra. Your
primary sign is ruled by Mercury, and Libra is ruled by
Venus, making for an excellent astrological combination,
and endowing you with both intellectual qualities, as well
as artistic and cultural interests.

You are an elegant Virgo due to the influence of Libra, but you also have a shrewd and analytical mind, with great powers of perception and intuition. These combined influences provide you with considerable luck because you have the best of both worlds: namely, the mental and the emotional.

To explain a little about Libra is important, because it will show how you have many of the traits of that star sign. First and foremost, Libra needs to be seen to be beautiful and acceptable. Coupled with your predisposition to be highly self-critical (particularly regarding minor personality flaws), this means that you could constantly struggle to be accepted by others—not because they don't like you, but because you have a flawed perception of how they see you. Try to accept yourself for who you are, and others will naturally accept you as well.

You're attracted to beautiful things and are, quite likely, a sensual and loving person. You have exotic tastes and love the best in furnishings. As far as personal grooming is concerned, you have a knack for looking very smart and elegant, but never overdo it with gaudy attire.

You have a great imagination, but have a tendency to stick to yourself. Some people might think you're elitist and are snubbing your nose at them, which is why you need to prove them wrong. You could show more of the aspects of your personality that are kind, caring and service-oriented. Others will soon realise that their initial judgement of you may have been rather harsh.

*You need to be surrounded by quiet and soothing
things. You like to have people in your life who
understand you, are peaceful by nature, and who
share some of the artistic and cultural interests that
you have.*

Being ruled by Venus makes you prone to overindulge
in pleasure, food and other activities in life. But because
Mercury is a sensitive planet, you need to be on guard
against overdoing things, and be sure to regulate your
life with discipline.

VIRGO CELEBRITIES

FAMOUS MALE:
HUGH GRANT

Humour is one of the best expressions of your ruling planet, Mercury. Born under your star sign is Hugh Grant, who exhibits this element of Mercury perfectly in the characters he plays on screen.

Hugh Grant, now a superstar in Hollywood, was born on the 9th of September, 1960, in England. Some of his best roles are in *Notting Hill*, where he played opposite Julia Roberts, and in *Music and Lyrics*, opposite Drew Barrymore. In both of these films he expresses the rather cautious, shy and at times awkward traits of Virgo, along with an interesting, dry humour that has become his trademark. Yes, this blend of characteristics is a perfect expression of Virgo.

His strive for perfection would find expression in his work as an actor, and although he makes acting seem easy, I can assure you that, with his Virgo Sun, he would struggle by being highly critical of his own performances. The painstaking attitude towards perfecting his craft paid off in 1994 when he won a Golden Globe Award for acting opposite Andie MacDowell in *Four Weddings and a Funeral*.

The following quote from Hugh makes me smile, because part of it does indeed express the Virgo temperament: 'I think film acting is just a miserable experience. It's so long and so boring and so difficult to get right so that what you need above all is incredible willpower and strength of mind.' Yes, the fact that he finds it difficult to get it right is what leads me to say that Hugh is significantly Virgo by nature.

Here is a self-confessed, 'committed and passionate perfectionist' on the filmset and, in his own words, a reluctant actor. According to him, he drifted into the role as a joke at the age of 23, and believes that it's unbecoming of a man growing older to be involved in this sort of work. Wow! Such a success, yet talking like this and humbling himself is such a Virgo trait.

HUGH AND HIS BAFTA

Hugh received a BAFTA award for Best Actor.
It's through the period of 1994 that he was
able to present himself as highly original
and clever in the way that he portrayed his
characters.

Jupiter, the exceptionally beneficial and lucky planet, transits Hugh's career zone during 2012. This indicates a whole range of opportunities and relationships opening up for him. He can achieve even greater heights in his success, but he must also be careful not to bite off more than he can chew.

FAMOUS FEMALE:
JADA PINKETT SMITH

Jada Pinkett Smith was born the 18th of September, 1971, in Baltimore, Maryland. This makes her a true Virgo, but with the cuspal influence of Libra as well. (Please read the earlier cusp information to find out more about this.)

As a result of having the combined influence of Mercury and Venus, it comes as no surprise that Jada excelled in dance and theatre at the Baltimore School for the Arts. She graduated in 1989, but continued her education at the North Carolina School of the Arts. For some reason she dropped out, and eventually moved to Los Angeles to pursue her dream of being an actress.

She looked for jobs in choreography and applied for the television series, *In Living Color*. She was unsuccessful in that, but fortunately befriended a talent agent and began her career in acting in 1990, initially starring in *Moe's World*. Although that didn't hit the screens and simply remained a pilot, she was fortunate enough to guest star in other shows as *True Colors*, *Doogie Howser, M.D.* and *21 Jump Street*.

JADA'S SUCCESS

*Her big breakthrough came in 1995 when she
starred with Eddie Murphy in the 1996 movie
The Nutty Professor. This was a huge success
at the box office and catapulted her into
international stardom.*

Jada's Virgo selflessness and dedication to an ideal is seen in her charity work and political interests. She's created the Will and Jada Smith Family Foundation in Baltimore, and she focuses her attention on the youth of urban cities, offering her support and advice, as well as money, to the cause.

Jada sums up her personal life philosophy in the following: 'I think women who lead full lives are better mothers'. This again highlights the Virgo woman's desire to serve as a mother, and as a fellow human being to anyone who wants help.

VIRGO
AT LARGE

MOST OF THE SHADOWS OF THIS
LIFE ARE CAUSED BY OUR STANDING
IN OUR OWN SUNSHINE.

Ralph Waldo Emerson

VIRGO MAN

♂

VIRGO MAN: SNAPSHOT

Intellectual

Perfectionist

Service-oriented

Shy

Clean

The Virgo man is an intellectual sort of character, thoroughly ruled by the planet Mercury. The penetrating and speedy action of this planet is clearly seen in him, and if you are reading this and are born under the sign of the Virgin, you'll know what I mean when I talk about the repetitiveness of our thinking processes.

You quickly grasp not just the superficialities of a situation, person or problem, but are also able to read between the lines, see beneath the surface, and gain insights into the hidden aspects of a situation. This is a distinct advantage, but it has its downsides as well. Let me explain.

In seeing things that others don't, you may sometimes be regarded as a nitpicker: someone who's uptight and hell-bent on imposing their sense of perfectionism on everyone.

But that's not at all how you see things, is it? You are simply committed to doing a job well, to improving a situation or a relationship, and, if and when you see a situation that needs rectifying, you're the first to call it as it is. Others who are not quite as insightful may not trust you, and this can create barriers between you.

In my experience of the Virgo man, I have found it difficult for people, in particular women, to get a clear handle on who you are. This may have much to do with the fact that your ruling planet Mercury is a dual/convertible planet, with one side of it clearly observable while the other is hidden.

In this respect, you may surprise others by never revealing some part of your personality, only to surprise them with it in a new set of circumstances. You use this as a form of control over others, because the element of surprise does have some function in dealing with power, doesn't it?

This is a very important part of your reading. It gives you hints as to how you should perhaps compromise with others to find a happy balance between realising your own ideals and fulfilling the needs of others. Yes, the word compromise does indeed seem to fit with the needs of Virgo in terms of fulfilment in life.

Sometimes, your fastidiousness and love of cleanliness and hygiene can get on other people's nerves. There may be rituals associated with how you go about your day-to-day life, which for you, are part of your normal, orderly routine. However, others may regard you as an obsessive-compulsive person in some respects

If you don't have to live with these people, there's no problem in being like this. However, getting married or flatting with someone may reveal such differences in style, and problems will arise. Pay attention to your rituals, and, again, try to find a happy medium between what you want and what others need, so that you can coexist peacefully.

Although on the surface you seem emotionally cold, this is only because you believe pragmatism is the safest way to make as few errors as possible in life. By getting a clear perspective through facts and figures, you come to your life decisions in ways that don't create emotional clouds. This is efficient living to you.

Idealist Virgo

Reliability, dedication to an ideal and perfecting your own inner self are all very high on the male Virgo agenda. However, these standards are often so out of reach for others that you may find yourself living alone, at home, disconnected from those who can't or won't live up to your expectations.

In friendship, you are a little reluctant to give away too much, and usually have only a few close friends whom you trust. You continue to hold back on your emotions because, primarily, you are an intellectual. Trusting others doesn't come easily, and people in your life must understand that it takes a good deal of time for you to open up completely.

VIRGO WOMAN

VIRGO WOMAN: SNAPSHOT

Trustworthy

Loyal

Practical

Fussy

Nervous

You are a woman born under the sign of Virgo. This is the pristine, virginal sign of the zodiac, indicating purity, cleanliness and deep understanding as the all-important motives in your relationships.

There are times when you do not trust others, and this is partly because you are apprehensive about letting yourself go. Could it be that you lack confidence in yourself and your ability to make the right judgements about others?

You're self-analytical and, due to the very powerful influence of Mercury on your personality, you're constantly analysing yourself and others, studying your shortcomings and trying to gain insight into how you can best live your life and improve your relationships.

In your attempts to perfect these aspects of your personality, you often find yourself becoming hyper-critical of yourself and those you love most. Yes, your motives are pure, but if people don't understand what is driving you, this could only serve to push them further and further away.

On the other hand, you are unassuming. People find you a great person to be around because you are usually cheerful, and you genuinely offer help and support in your friendships and family life. You are efficient in everything you do and especially in the way you conduct your work. You're always there to lend a hand, and not necessarily because you want anything in return. I would even go so far as to say that, along with the signs of Cancer and Pisces, Virgo is the most self-effacing and self-sacrificial sign of the zodiac. The term 'unconditional love' truly applies to many born under the sign of Virgo, especially if they are women.

Because you want everything to be just right, those with whom you live and work need to understand that your approach to getting things done properly can, alas, take you much longer than the rest of us. If people are impatient, it can present challenges and problems for you.

It's a difficult thing for the Virgo woman to compromise her standards for the sake of meeting a deadline. Although you are a thinker and tend to reason things out, this in no way makes you impractical. Quite the opposite, actually. You are the sort of person who thinks along practical lines. You are the supreme pragmatist who only sees value in an idea if it can be materially implemented and exploited.

You're constantly second-guessing yourself on your abilities, however, and even though you may be highly accomplished in a field, there's always something within you that creates considerable self-distrust. You have great abilities in both the arts and the sciences, and many born under Virgo spend not only their work time but their personal time investigating and enjoying these aspects of life. You may even be someone who can play an instrument or easily dabble in fine arts or other crafts. You love to use your hands.

No one, for a minute, should believe they can pull the wool over the eyes of a Virgo woman. You have an incredible memory due to your highly developed mental region. Mercury enables you to intuitively grasp what others are saying and what their true personalities are, and allows you to go back into your memory banks to retrieve information in a split second. This can be rather daunting to others if they think they've got you wrapped around their little finger. We both know that isn't the case!

Helping others is a key to finding satisfaction in your life. You find life meaningless if you're simply living it for yourself. This is why you are an excellent mother and provider for your home and family. There's nothing more satisfying than seeing that you've actually rendered assistance to someone in need and that your advice, always practical, has been accepted and implemented with good results.

Indecision is usually relegated to the signs of Gemini and Libra, but there are some Virgo women who tend to oscillate in their opinions and can't come to a conclusion.

Once again, this comes back to trust—both in yourself and in the processes of life.

Don't get too bogged down in the intellectual aspects of a situation, but use your heart along with your head to draw the correct conclusions.

VIRGO CHILD

There are pros and cons to being ruled by the planet Mercury, and in the case of a Virgo child, it's a delicate balance. The high energy of this planet can deteriorate into nervousness that creates emotional and physical problems for the young child of Virgo, and is something that should be monitored closely by their parents.

Mercury governs the nervous system, and being fully activated in the horoscope of Virgo youngsters, makes them prone to nervous disorders, hypochondria and even attention-deficit disorders. Their minds are sometimes scattered from having too much mental energy at their disposal.

Parents of a Virgo child can help by taking control of situations quickly, and offering them a steady yet guiding hand to give them a sense of comfort and perfection, and develop self-confidence. If you give your Virgo child something constructive to do with their energy, then boredom and psychological problems will be dovetailed into practical outlets.

An important point—and one that should be driven home—is that it's okay to simply enjoy the moment and not be overly concerned if the results are not exactly right.

Because your Virgo child may not always articulate what's on their mind, you mustn't assume that everything is running smoothly in their world. You should frequently quiz them, talk to them and get them to develop the art of opening up and expressing their feelings from an early age. It'll help them in later life.

Although at times the predominating influence of Mercury makes them persistent chatterboxes, try to make yourself available as much as possible to share in their discussions, which are all-important to them.

The other thing that will both amuse and exasperate you is their unending stream of questions. Curiosity is one of the key attributes of children born under Virgo, so be prepared to answer each and every detailed inquiry on this, that and the other. You may even need to a have a book of facts, answers and general knowledge at your fingertips to answer questions that prove to be out of your league.

Fun Virgo

You'll have a lot of fun with your Virgo child, and may even find yourself mentally stimulated into a more knowledgeable phase of your own life by having them around.

Finally, Virgo children need a tidy, comfortable environment in which to work—and work they will. Even at a young age, your little Virgo will be a tireless worker and may place undue pressure on him or herself when it comes to schoolwork. You'd better help them through this, and above all, help them maintain an organised diary so that they know exactly what they need to do and when. This will go a long way to reducing any tension in their lives.

VIRGO LOVER

If you're a guy who is reading this, perhaps simply to find out the best way to seduce your newly found Virgo girlfriend, you need to understand that she's a modest woman who's not at all quick to draw romantic conclusions of any kind. If you're after a quick fix, let me say that the Virgo girl is the wrong woman for you.

In my years of research into the Virgo woman, I have found they are more practical than sexual—but don't let that lead you to believe that a Virgo female is passionless. Not so. What I'm saying is that the female Virgo is simply slow to loosen the grip on her heart before handing it over to a deserving partner.

Unfortunately, when it comes to love, Virgo can be a little cold and analytical in trying to understand the other person's feelings and motives as well as their own. You may feel as though you are being judged and under the microscope more often than not. Well, you'll just need to be on your best behaviour, won't you, and offer Virgo something more than the average person out there. Are you up to the task?

The other important point to make is that Virgo is one of the most loyal star signs. Once they give their heart to someone, even under the most trying of circumstances, that commitment will not be shaken.

Virginal Virgo?

The Virgin of Virgo misrepresents the deeper passion and selfless love that Virgos indeed bring to relationships with those who are patient enough to have this revealed to them. Virgo is playful, passionate and intensely curious when it comes to lovemaking, but only under the right circumstances.

Virgos are reluctant to leave a relationship, especially once they've invested time, energy and emotion into the partnership. Just as they are prudent with money, they are prudent with their emotional investments, and want to see the best possible returns. I know this sounds rather mercenary, but practicality seems to be a cornerstone of their approach to relationships as well.

In a relationship with a Virgo, you need to captivate their attention. Their Mercurial minds are ever changing, ever desirous of variety and intellectual stimulation. If you're a couch potato and spend your days watching television in an uncommunicative state, Virgo will not consider you to be the right match. Communication, expression and the exchange of ideas and information is the bedrock of a successful relationship with those born under the virginal sign of Virgo.

Modest but Passionate Virgo

Don't let the shy exterior of Virgo fool you. Mercury, their ruler, is hot, and you'll be surprised to experience that passion of theirs in the bedroom. But first win their trust!

VIRGO FRIEND

Only a few people can live up to a Virgo's set of standards when it comes to friendship. So, consider yourself lucky if you can include at least one Virgo in your trusted social circle.

The caring attitude of Virgo, and the way in which they're always ready to lend a helping hand, is probably the most notable quality in their friendship. But it's not a one-way street. While they have great concern for your wellbeing, you must at least show a little affection and kindness in return. Yes, the Virgo friend is unconditional in their friendship. Yes, the Virgo friend is unconditional in their love. But remember that it's nice to be loved back, too.

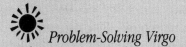

Problem-Solving Virgo

In terms of helping others with their problems, this is an area in which Virgo excels. They have the uncanny ability to dissect a problem practically, to accurately assess the situation with all the subtle factors that comprise it, and give you an extremely detailed breakdown, leading to a simple solution. Interestingly, they are impartial in the way they do this.

You'll need to get used to the fact that Virgo doesn't mince words when it comes to giving an opinion, especially when asked. They are honest and generous to a fault, and so are rather blunt in pointing out your shortcomings. They are highly critical, and can sometimes shock you with the manner in which they candidly expose you and others.

You can now see, from my description of your Virgo friend, that truth is a double-edged sword for both of you. Their honesty lays bare the good, the bad and the ugly. Even if you find them cold and sometimes emotionally disconnected from a situation, it's only because they are trying to step back and not allow their emotions to be unduly coloured by the circumstances. To them (or to you, Virgo, if you're reading this), being clear, truthful and unaffected by superfluous issues is important for getting to the bottom of an issue.

They look towards perfection in their search for friends, and you'll find them eclectic in that they appreciate many different viewpoints, even if they don't necessarily adhere to those philosophies. They love variety and, in social circumstances, can be really interesting to have around. When they're relaxed they can be a lot of fun. Having the quick and humorous Mercury as their ruler helps them enjoy a good laugh when the time is right.

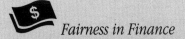

Fairness in Finance

You mustn't take liberties with your Virgo friend, especially when it comes to money. They are careful and calculating in this area, and will only ever pay their fair share. Never try to deceive them financially, or their simple solution will be to disappear and never be seen again. Under those circumstances, it would be a shame to lose your Virgo friend, for they can be a trusted, lifelong ally.

VIRGO ENEMY

It's hard to know when you've made an enemy of Virgo, because although they are very intelligent and communicative, they are known to withhold and not necessarily communicate all of the negative points that are on their mind.

The first hint that you've made your Virgo friend an enemy is that they become extremely cold and distant. 'Shutdown mode' is usually the first stage of Virgo becoming your enemy.

If this is happening, some of the questions you may ask yourself could relate to your trustworthiness, dependability, or saying something that has insulted or disrespected them in public. Humiliating a Virgo is really a no-no.

Vehement Virgo

If you've indeed made an enemy of Virgo, and they're ready to voice their opinion, prepare for a scathing attack that will strip you down to your bare bones and expose all the aspects of your personality that are inappropriate or contradictory. The Virgo individual can be rather vehement when it comes to speaking their mind.

If you're thinking of making up with Virgo, communication— preceded by a sincere apology—is the first step.

VIRGO
AT HOME

IT'S BETTER TO BE AN AUTHENTIC
LOSER THAN A FALSE SUCCESS, AND
TO DIE ALIVE THAN TO LIVE DEAD.

William Markiewicz

HOME FRONT

Because Virgo is an earth sign, you can rest assured that, the dwelling place of those born under the Virgin sign will be an unpretentious, natural and comfortable to live in.

 Earthy Virgo

Anything associated with the earth, including plants, rocks, crystals, fresh air and sunlight, will make up your living space, Virgo. And as a result of this, visitors to your home will feel extremely comfortable, relaxed and open.

This down-to-earth, no-nonsense approach to your house and decoration conveys a simplicity and orderliness that makes you feel comfortable, but, at times, it may glaringly show up the deficiencies in your visitors' own living styles.

This is particularly so if you're an extreme Virgo who, for example, likes to cover their furniture with sheets, cover their carpets with plastic mats, and dust each and every nook and cranny so that there is an almost sterile finish to the place. If possible, try to avoid such obsessiveness, and get rid of the plastic and white sheets. Furniture is meant to be lived in, felt and experienced.

You crave simplicity, and have a conservative approach towards furnishings. Because you like to do a lot of work and are creative, there may be computers and other work-related materials scattered throughout your house. But, as always, organisation, the methodical placement of objects, and tidiness will be that on which you base the arrangement of your furnishings and the way you live.

You feel uncomfortable if people are uneasy, so you do your best to entertain family and guests in a selfless manner. You are extremely courteous, but do it in an unpretentious way, which is why visitors to the house of a Virgo feel so welcome.

Earthy colours, including green, brown, sand, and also wheat and wood blends, are excellent for relaxing you. Natural materials, such as timber, stone and, of course, a garden environment as an extension to your living space, all make sense for those of you born under Virgo.

It's important that you don't overdo the detail and perfectionism in the way you design and lay out your house. This might not work well with some of the more natural, earthy and 'hang loose' feelings that these textures and materials offer you.

Dirt Alert

Virgo loves hygiene and cleanliness at all times. If you live with a Virgo, clean up occasionally, and watch their face light up!

KARMA, LUCK AND MEDITATION

Virgos usually find their luck through slow and steady, patient action. But luck may not always occur suddenly or quickly. You mustn't rely on others for your success, but rather on your own efforts and intuition. Even if what is offered to you seems like a gift on a silver plate, you just don't trust that success could come quite so easily.

Saturn rules your zone of past karma and good fortune. Because of this, you may need to wait until later in life to access your karmic fruits. The good luck you receive will sometimes be the result of extra hard work, and possibly even challenges and obstacles that others don't experience. Such is the influence of Saturn on your life.

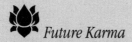

Future Karma

Your future karma and what is likely to happen in your life are ruled by Virgo and Mercury. Mercury is a lucky planet that indicates a bright future if you communicate openly and don't bottle up your emotions. Work with this planet and that principle to free up lucky vibrations, which will come back to you as success, wealth and good relationships.

'I Serve' is your life phrase. Try to become more aware of your own needs as distinct from what others demand of you. You must develop your self-esteem in line with the idea that you, too, are worthy of being served and supported in life. This is the best way for Virgo to become self-empowered, find peace of mind and achieve superior happiness.

Wednesdays, Fridays and Saturdays are lucky for your emotional healing and self-development. Spend a little time each day doing something spontaneous that you wouldn't normally do. This will augment your luck.

Lucky Days

Your luckiest days are Wednesday, Friday and Saturday.

Lucky Numbers

Lucky numbers for Virgo include the following. You may wish to experiment with these in lotteries and other games of chance:

6, 15, 24, 33, 42, 51

5, 14, 23, 32, 41, 50

8, 17, 26, 35, 44, 53

Destiny Years

The most significant years in your life are likely to be 5, 14, 23, 32, 41, 50, 68, 77 and 86.

HEALTH, WELLBEING AND DIET

The sixth sign of the zodiac, Virgo, governs health and disease. For this reason, you also have a natural affinity with the concepts of feeling good and looking after your health and wellbeing.

You are a sensitive individual because your nervous system is very finely tuned and developed. You feel much more than others, and can be vulnerable to the negative influences of the people with whom you live, play and work. It's therefore important, as a primary prerequisite for maintaining good health, that you associate only with people who are going to make you feel good about yourself.

Environmentally speaking, you regularly need to look at what could be disturbing influences on you. It may benefit you to allow yourself sufficient space and give yourself mental room to breathe. If you're dissatisfied with those with whom you work or live, this will impact dramatically on your health. You need to eliminate any negative factors that could undermine your emotional wellbeing.

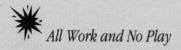

All Work and No Play

Overworking is an activity that sometimes catches out the Virgo native. Temper your work practices, get adequate sleep, and don't live on your nerves.

The digestive system is ruled by Virgo so what you eat and, more importantly, how you eat it, is essential in avoiding discomfort and disease in your body. You must listen to your body signals when they say that a certain food or activity does not agree with you.

Eat in a relaxed state of mind, and carefully study the sorts of foods that are agreeable to you or otherwise. Many Virgos I have found develop strong allergic reactions to foods because they can be so hypersensitive. Once you regularly do this analysis for yourself, you'll discover what foods are aggravating you.

In dietary terms, you must always supplement natural, wholesome foods with herbs like skull-cap, chamomile, vervain and valerian root, to keep your nerves in a strong and stable state. Vitamins B, C and E, along with whole grains such as rye, wheat and barley, are also important components of your diet to keep you healthy. Don't forget the green vegetables because according to ancient astrologists, Mercury, which rules your sign, is a green colour.

FINANCE FINESSE

You are primarily concerned about how best to perform your work rather than constantly harping on about how much you will get for what you do. This is due to the fact that you are a committed worker, are practical, and are great at what you do.

You like to feel as if you deserve what you earn, and don't feel comfortable if haven't worked your hardest to reward yourself.

Venus and Libra govern your finances and, in particular, your earnings and money generally. You love to have things, but only if they are useful—you hate to buy things that remain useless. If you do so, it will seem as if the money could have been more wisely spent elsewhere.

You are sensible in your spending, which is why you are able to save money, but at the same time you still appear lavish in your habits. You spend wisely and always look for a bargain.

 Financial Fortune

Venus shows you can earn well and invest in refined things like art, furnishings and other valuable aesthetic objects like sculptures and antiques. Because Venus is fortunate in most matters, you will most likely enjoy amassing a good deal of money at some stage.

VIRGO
AT WORK

IT'S A RARE THING TO FIND
SOMEBODY YOU CAN WORK WITH,
WORK OFF OF, AND HAVE FUN WITH.

Matthew Ashford

VIRGO CAREER

IDEAL PROFESSIONS

Healthcare professional

Social worker

Dietician

Accountant

Research analyst

Teacher

Executive or personal assistant

As your star sign is the sixth of the zodiac, which naturally rules the area of work and daily routine, Virgo and work are almost synonymous. It is important for you to find a job that is meaningful and gives you the opportunity to express yourself at the deepest level, otherwise you'll never be quite fulfilled. Finding meaningful employment, working in a way that allows you to perfect your ideas and to produce good, clean and useful work for your employers and clients, is your aim in life.

You take your work seriously and employ much of your intellectual abilities in whatever it is that you do. Money is important to you, of course, being an earth sign, but not as important as a job well done. You're not the type of person to look at the clock every five minutes and ask, 'When is this going to be over?' Getting lost in your work and perfecting what has been allotted to you is the way in which you prefer to work.

Because you're so detailed in your analysis, your organisational skills will be great, but they could suffer if you haven't set up a plan to allocate and delegate some tasks to others. You're great with people and communicate well, and, as such, you'd make a great teacher, scientist or logician in one of the deductive sciences.

Your problem-solving skills are highly developed, and you can apply them to such things as customer care, service support, human resources and industrial relations.

Just remember to work in an environment that is going to allow you to express your inner self harmoniously, and to do work that is meaningful. As a result, you'll surely achieve success and happiness in your working life.

Uranus

Your workplace planet is Uranus. What does this mean for you professionally? Because Uranus is so unpredictable, your work efforts are sometimes interfered with by forces outside of your control. These will tend to cause problems for your health as well. Maintain an optimistic view of life, and don't overwork.

Mercury

Mercury, your career ruler, makes you quick in thought, versatile, and a master of communication. Any career that gives you the chance to express your communicative and service skills will fulfil you professionally and bring you success.

VIRGO BOSS

First and foremost, you must understand that your Virgo boss is probably vulnerable in certain areas, particularly if he or she has taken on a large part of the business and hasn't yet delegated many tasks. By understanding that they are not necessarily well suited to a high-powered executive role, you can gently coax them into delegating some of those tasks to you, which will, in turn, relieve their mental and nervous strain. You will quickly become their favourite employee.

Your Virgo boss painstakingly analyses everything. Once they've drawn a conclusion, it will be difficult for you to change their mind. It is far better for you to get involved earlier in the process when, notwithstanding his or her super critical attitude, they may still listen to good advice, especially if it's logical and practical.

There's clarity in the way your boss runs the company, and they need the time and support from others to make their vision a reality. However, you must accept that things may not happen too quickly, because every detail must be dealt with systematically. In the extreme, your Virgo boss could become a ditherer, going around and around, trying to analyse and deduct rather than ever implementing what is being studied.

This is where, as an employee, a friend, or even a relative of the Virgo boss, you'll need to gently goad them into making a decision and accepting the results with a smile. Be truthful with your Virgo boss, even if what you tell them is not necessarily to their liking. You'll be respected for your honesty.

Dedication is another issue for Virgo. If their loyalty is undermined by hypocrites, you'll soon know about it. And don't for a minute think that your Virgo boss is going to overlook your mistakes and let them slide. They will be attentive to every finicky aspect of the tasks that have been allotted to you.

In the end, however, Virgos (and this includes those who are employers) have kind hearts, and like to be fair and judicious in the way they deal with their colleagues and employees.

They are dependable, and once they have given you their word, they will stick to their guns. They really do want to help you, and this is born from their inbuilt attribute of compassion.

VIRGO EMPLOYEE

 Meticulous Employee

The nice thing about Virgo is that they genuinely don't want to outshine others. They are happy to do their work as meticulously as possible and see that, in the larger context, their contributions are going to make a difference. Service is their key word, and perfection in that service is the supporting attribute of their make-up.

If you've hired a Virgo employee, you should get used to a few things. First and foremost, Virgo never rushes a job. If you overload them with too many tasks and demand that they finish these too quickly, this will jeopardise the quality of their work, and leave them feeling very unfulfilled.

That isn't desirable. Instead, try to plan your work schedule with them, to gain an understanding of what they will need to feel that the work they do is up to their standards and expectations. Please note, if you are an employer, that Virgo's standards will probably be much higher than yours, so there's nothing to worry about as far as quality or service is concerned.

However, one issue you may encounter will be that of time. Somewhere between the poles of time and quality you'll find a happy medium, and you'll be glad you did because your Virgo employee is very hard to replace if you lose them.

Learn to use some of the skills that your Virgo employee has as a natural part of their character: use their analytical abilities to help you, and let them express some of their concepts on a creative level—they actually have a very refined and eclectic taste. Discrimination, too, is another important attribute of Virgo, which helps them make the right decisions.

You can give your Virgo employee a variety of tasks, and this is good because it will keep them mentally active and interested. They are curious and adaptable to both their workload and any changing environments in which you put them. They are clear-headed, intelligent and reliable, and as I said earlier, one thing you can look forward to is not receiving sloppy and untidy work from them. They are patient and meticulous, and they finish whatever task has been assigned to them.

SERVICE AND CUSTOMER CARE

Service and customer care areas are ideal work options for a Virgo employee. They are very conscious about being helpful, and it's likely they lead a rather clean life, rest adequately, and take care to provide consistent and dependable service to their employers.

As an advertisement for your business, Virgo's neat and understated attire will hold you in good stead, reflecting some of the conservative but service-oriented aspects of what you're trying to deliver to customers. You can trust your business in the hands of your Virgo employee.

PROFESSIONAL RELATIONSHIPS: BEST AND WORST

BEST PAIRING:
VIRGO AND CAPRICORN

What a fabulous business combination this is! It's like the proverbial hand in glove: a perfect fit. And once again, the reason for this is, of course, the beautiful blending of the well-grounded temperaments of earth signs.

The first thing you will notice—and most likely respect—in the Capricorn with whom you work is their serious approach, their dedication to an ideal, no matter how long it takes, and the precision with which they go about their tasks.

Does this sound familiar? It should, Virgo, because in many ways you are exactly like this, too. Capricorn's approach to work is not unlike yours. You can both synchronise your activities and proceed in a similar fashion.

If I try to look back at all the Capricorns I know and have known, including my grandmother, one thing stands out: how very economical they are. And I have met many Virgos who are also able to stretch a dollar quite cleverly. The combined economic attitudes that you bring to a professional relationship, especially if you are planning an independent business, will be a distinct bonus.

You support each other well, and never take advantage of financial or material aspects. You both hate waste and too often this is an overlooked principle when running a business. Success is not only based how much you earn, but on how much you are able to save, and by how much you can reduce your losses. The Virgo-Capricorn combination is perfect in a climate that requires frugal attitudes.

The only thing that may hold you back a little, notwithstanding how great this combination is, is Capricorn's often overly serious moods. You may have to use a little of that quirky Virgo humour to lift them out of the doldrums, if you can.

WORST PAIRING: VIRGO AND PISCES

The opposition of the earth and water signs found in the Virgo and Pisces combination makes it a complicated match. Yes, earth and water do mix, but the muddy quality that results doesn't give us much hope, especially if financial elements are involved.

Virgo's practicality is necessary for the stable functioning of any business enterprise. By the same token, the emotional and intuitive/creative components of the

Pisces' temperament can propel ventures to the heights of glory with wonderful ideas that convince the masses to part with their money.

So essentially, the two of you possess the individual skills to create something wonderful. It's in their implementation—the coming together, and the resolution of these ideas into a workable plan—where your relationship will fall down.

Virgo, you want to own every last detail of the plan, however insignificant it may be, which means that, at times, you are incapable of delegating. You mustn't apply your microscope to the Piscean work ethic, because they will see this as a form of mistrust. Unfortunately, though, you can't help yourself. The dreamy (what you would call impractical) Pisces irritates you, and makes you feel so nervous that you will not be able to achieve your objectives.

But not all Pisces have their heads in the clouds permanently. Behind the vacant, at times glazed look is a mind and imagination that is working overtime to produce something that is not only commercially viable, but that can transform people, and perhaps even add a greater dimension to the human experience as a whole.

It is not likely that the Virgo and Pisces match on a business level will have much going for it, but if it's the choice you have made, your sharp criticism should most certainly be toned down with your Pisces partner.

VIRGO
IN LOVE

DON'T LET SOMEONE BE A PRIORITY
IN YOUR LIFE WHEN YOU ARE JUST
AN OPTION IN THEIRS.

Anonymous

ROMANTIC COMPATIBILITY

How compatible are you with your current partner, lover or friend? Did you know that astrology can reveal a whole new level of understanding between people, simply by looking at their star sign and that of their partner? I'd like to share some special insights that will help you better appreciate your strengths and challenges using Sun sign compatibility.

The Sun reflects your drive, willpower and personality. The essential qualities of two star signs blend like two pure colours that produce an entirely new colour. Relationships, similarly, produce their own emotional colours when two people interact. The following section is a general guide to your romantic prospects with others and how, by knowing the astrological 'colour' of each other, the art of love can help you create a masterpiece.

Each of the twelve star signs has a greater or lesser affinity with the others. The two quick-reference tables will show you who's hot and who's not as far as your relationships are concerned.

The Star Sign Compatibility table rates your chance as a percentage of general compatibility, while the Horoscope Compatibility table summarises the reasons why. The results of each star sign combination are also listed.

When reading I ask you to remember that no two star signs are ever *totally* incompatible. With effort and compromise, even the most difficult astrological matches can work. Don't close your mind to the full range of life's possibilities! Learning about each other and ourselves is the most important facet of astrology.

Good luck in your search for love, and may the stars shine upon you in 2012!

STAR SIGN COMPATIBILITY
FOR LOVE AND FRIENDSHIP
(PERCENTAGES)

	Aries	Taurus	Gemini	Cancer	Leo	Virgo	Libra	Scorpio	Sagittarius	Capricorn	Aquarius	Pisces
Aries	60	65	65	65	90	45	70	80	90	50	55	65
Taurus	60	70	70	80	70	90	75	85	50	95	80	85
Gemini	70	70	75	60	80	75	90	60	75	50	90	50
Cancer	65	80	60	75	70	75	60	95	55	45	70	90
Leo	90	70	80	70	85	75	65	75	95	45	70	75
Virgo	45	90	75	75	75	70	80	85	70	95	50	70
Libra	70	75	90	60	65	80	80	85	80	85	95	50
Scorpio	80	85	60	95	75	85	85	90	80	65	60	95
Sagittarius	90	50	75	55	95	70	80	85	85	55	60	75
Capricorn	50	95	50	45	45	95	85	65	55	85	70	85
Aquarius	55	80	90	70	70	50	95	60	60	70	80	55
Pisces	65	85	50	90	75	70	50	95	75	85	55	80

In the compatibility table above please note that some compatibilities have seemingly contradictory ratings. Why you ask? Well, remember that no two people experience the relationship in exactly the same way. For one person a relationship may be more advantageous, more supportive than for the other. Sometimes one gains more than the other partner and therefore the compatibility rating will be higher for them.

HOROSCOPE COMPATIBILITY FOR VIRGO

Virgo with		Romance/Sexual
Aries	👎	Disappointing match because you are not particularly fulfilled by Aries
Taurus	☀️	Truly one of the great combinations of the zodiac, a wonderful love match
Gemini	❤️‍🔥	Your sexual and mental connection is very stimulating!
Cancer	💘	Wonderful relationship if you can deal with Cancer's moodiness
Leo	☠️	Leos are too demanding of you, and you're too demanding of them!

	Friendship		Professional
✗	The lack of sensitivity and grace by Aries annoys you	✗	Intellectual clashes and unbridled arguments make this combination a no-go
✔	Taurus is forbearing and can handle you more easily than most	✔	A practical, somewhat reserved match that is always concerned about future security
✔	Gemini is stimulating to your imagination and spirit	✔	Gemini's curious and inventive mind is a great fit for your professional aspirations—try tying them down, though!
✔	Excellent friendship that can last	✔	You can profitably engage with a Cancer, but don't be too critical
✗	Some good and bad points for friendship; a middling chance	✗	Leo will feel constrained by your constant need for detailed analysis—not the best match

Virgo with		Romance/Sexual
Virgo		Selfless and loving relationship, making it a good match
Libra		Libra is too spontaneous and easygoing for you, and their large social circle may intimidate you
Scorpio		Excellent sexual connection that enlivens your sensual nature
Sagittarius		Sagittarius's big-picture approach versus Virgo's micro-analyses disturbs your relationship
Capricorn		Cautious Capricorn still knows how to share their emotions and their sexuality with you—a good match

	Friendship		Professional
✗	Great intellectual rapport but you may start to see flaws in each other's personalities	✔	Both frugal and therefore excellent at saving money; don't be too cautious
✔	An interesting if not unique combination of energies, much intellectual rapport between the two of you	✗	Expensive combination, and it's hard for you to keep a tally of Libra's activities
✔	A good tag team— Scorpio can be confrontational, but you are able to handle them	✔	Both of you are good with money, so this is a pairing that promises a lucrative future
✗	Adventure-seeking Sagittarius will offer you a fun time, but you must be prepared to let go	✗	Where did all the money go? Answer: you got into business with Sagittarius
✔	Once Capricorn trusts you enough they will open their heart to you	✔	Where did all this money come from? Answer: you are in business with Capricorn

Virgo with		Romance/Sexual
Aquarius	♥	Unusual relationship that will not flow easily; sex and intimacy don't gel
Pisces	♥	Opposites don't always attract, loving Pisces doesn't understand your clinical approach to love

Friendship		Professional	
✗	Imposing your fussiness on Aquarius will see them turn their back on you—go easy, Virgo	✔	Your causes are practical, but Aquarius is a world revolutionary, so be prepared to spend your money on their causes
✗	You want Pisces to talk more, Pisces wants you to talk less—a no-go	✗	There is no way you will keep Pisces accountable—they fly by the seat of their pants while having their head in the clouds

VIRGO
PARTNERSHIPS

Virgo + Aries

Virgo is passionate but not overtly so, as Aries is, so this combination needs time for intimacy to develop. The primal and less-than-sensitive reactions of Aries will be a turn-off to you.

Virgo + Taurus

There's a strong link between you romantically, so I can safely predict your pleasure ratio will be high. You sexually balance and stimulate each other, and this is an area that should bring you great satisfaction as a couple.

Virgo + Gemini

Gemini will excite and stimulate you to explore different avenues, thereby bringing you closer together. It's probably not the most striking sexual combination, but is one that, with a little mutual affection, will grow in time.

Virgo + Cancer

You have a positive influence on each other and are better people for having met. Your personalities are truly compatible, so there's not much of a downside to this relationship.

Virgo + Leo

Leo is a dominating star sign, whereas you have a tendency to nitpick, which could cause tension. Give each other the space to be who you are and things should work quite well. If you know you are correct, sharpen your diplomatic skills for pointing out the errors of Leo's ways.

Virgo + Virgo

In your moments of intimacy and lovemaking, you'll have a similar approach and respect each other's need for good taste and sensitivity. You are emotional, but this is not immediately obvious. With another Virgo, it will be easier for you to feel understood.

Virgo + Libra

Libra loves sexuality and the idea of love and romance. Give them plenty of that and you will possess them. Libra likes to play the field, however, and may not be quite as committed as you are to the relationship.

 Virgo + Scorpio

A great match. However, dissatisfaction may sneak into the relationship, because both of you have high expectations of each other and can be somewhat demanding. It's a good idea to foster respect between you by allowing for some personal space and not judging too harshly.

 Virgo + Sagittarius

The way you love is poles apart from Sagittarius. Being the more reserved person, you're not likely give away too much. But by not expressing your emotions as openly as Sagittarius, they may misinterpret your inhibition as disinterest or snobbery. They prefer an experimental approach to lovemaking, which gives vent to their fiery urges.

Virgo + Capricorn

You enjoy a fine relationship with Capricorn and provide them with a little more pleasure than they are used to. Capricorn will slowly open up to your ways and will make you feel extremely secure about your future. They are hardworking and know how important material goals are to you.

Virgo + Aquarius

There is an idealistic connection between the two of you, possibly karmic. In time, you will combine your powers, perhaps to work for a greater cause. However, if you want this to succeed, you mustn't constantly superimpose your perfectionist attitudes on Aquarius.

Virgo + Pisces

Both your star signs are mutable, which means you're changeable and moody by nature. You'll try to understand Pisces with your mind, and they will try to intuit you with their emotions. This appears to be a relationship of parallel railway tracks: they travel in the same direction, but never quite come together.

PLATONIC RELATIONSHIPS: BEST AND WORST

BEST PAIRING: VIRGO AND TAURUS

If the general temperament of two people is compatible, then some of the minor nuances that irritate us can be accepted far more easily. This is the case with a platonic relationship between Virgo and Taurus.

This is an excellent combination because the two of you share the earth element, making you practical, somewhat reserved and always concerned about your future security. In Taurus you see an essential pragmatist: a person who can offer you the stability that you seek so much.

Taurus is grounded and neatly counteracts some of the more nervous and highly strung aspects of your personality. By spending time with a Taurus in social situations, and quiet moments over a coffee where you share your inner feelings and thoughts, you will find a great friend in the Bull.

You, Virgo, have a tendency to expect perfection in everything, and relationships and friendships are no exception. The Bull is forbearing, and can handle your comments far more easily than most, but you mustn't take this for granted. They have a limit to their patience, and when they blow their cool, they really blow.

As far as your lifestyle choices and interests are concerned, you both share the same ideals in art, music and even cooking and culinary events—indeed, you seem to reflect much of each other in your interests. This is truly one of the great combinations of the zodiac.

WORST PAIRING:
VIRGO AND AQUARIUS

In the Virgo and Aquarius platonic relationship, your experiences are kept in a cool and moderately contained emotional state. The two of you may find some common interests, particularly in the way you express yourselves. But being emotionally connected is a highly important part of any relationship, and this is where a friendship between the two of you might fall over, and get badly battered and bruised as a result.

It is best that you are involved when in a friendship, but it's not easy to overcome your insecurities or let go of yourself with an Aquarius. You need to look more at the similarities rather than the differences between you.

The common ideals between the two of you are those of service and humanitarianism. Your catchcry is 'I Serve', while Aquarius has an extended awareness that is inclusive of all people, thereby endowing him or her with a similar desire to serve the world. Try to focus on this rather than the different approaches you take to living your lives, following or not following the rules, and being conventional or otherwise.

If you are a Virgo who has just met an Aquarius, it is probably a good idea to keep them at arm's length until you can decide whether or not this sort of friendship is truly comfortable for you.

....

VIRGO AND AQUARIUS MAY NEVER AGREE

Virgo and Aquarius fall in inimical places to each other in the zodiac, indicating the absolutely incompatible nature of your star signs. Trying to connect with each other will be a difficult thing for both of you.

....

SEXUAL RELATIONSHIPS: BEST AND WORST

BEST PAIRING:
VIRGO AND SCORPIO

I'm going to tell you that the Virgo-Scorpio combination is the best for you, Virgo, even though some of you, including other astrologers, may argue with me.

At first, one might think of the water signs as being more conducive to chemistry in the bedroom, but I'm going to use a little bit of astrological licence and speak from a deeper level about this unusual combination.

Scorpio, the passionate and intense star sign of the zodiac, immediately feels intrigued by the shy and often coy Virgo. The fact that Scorpio can't possess you instantly is a turn-on in itself. Once you show some interest, those piercing scorpionic eyes will do their best to drill through those conservative layers of your mind and your heart.

Scorpio is intellectual and philosophical, and this will fascinate you. Their magnetic appeal is hard to resist, and there is something about you that attracts them. There's no doubt that a relationship between you gets the green light. I see compatibility mentally for you, and this is important because once the sexual excitement has waned, it's nice to know you will still have something else going on.

This kind of dynamic may make you feel uneasy, though. But you might also feel as if this person is genuinely trying to understand you and, of course, you interpret that to be an intellectual process. Let's not forget that Scorpio has at their disposal not just a penetrating intellect and deep, intense emotions, but, at times, crystal clear intuition as well.

The reason that this sexual relationship is so great is that the intellectual quality of Virgo and the emotional power of Scorpio strangely combine, and each of you is able to imbibe the qualities of the other.

Over time, this combination brings with it spiritual benefits, not just sexual, which is why I deem it to be on the top rung of compatibilities in the zodiac.

SEXUALLY DEMANDING

On the topic of sex, Scorpio can be a little more demanding than you care for. If you can get into the swing of their intense and passionate sexual habits, your relationship with them has an even greater chance of survival. You must understand that they are the most sexual of the star signs, and they need nourishment on that level. It's a big ask, Virgo.

You need to learn the art of feeling your inner being rather than continually overtaxing your mind with rational thinking. Scorpio is good for you this way. They can teach you to feel, to forget the intellectual process and all the self-consciousness that goes with it. All you need to do, Virgo, is trust your Scorpio friend, and experience the joy, love and physical fulfilment that comes from bonding with the Scorpion.

WORST PAIRING:
VIRGO AND ARIES

'Oh, my God! How did this happen?' We have to ask this, because the Virgin and the Ram have so little in common that it seems to be the most natural question.

You are probably feeling disappointed, Virgo, if you are already sexually involved with an Aries, but come on, fess up! You and I both know full well that you're not fulfilled by Aries, don't we?

Aries is hot, dynamic, spontaneous and extremely passionate. What's wrong with all of this? Isn't that what I want? Well, yes and no. Virgo is passionate, but not overtly so, as Aries is, so this combination needs time for intimacy to develop. The primal and often insensitive reactions of Aries can be distasteful to you. However, your lovemaking could become an educational experience. If your Aries partner is an intelligent person who enjoys communication, then the prognosis is much better.

The fire sign of Aries eventually melts earth, turning it into a liquidy molten lava, which flows, but is uncomfortable under that amount of heat. This is how Aries will grind you down. Often they lack the sensitivity and sentimental graces that you wish for in your love life.

Also, the impatient Aries, although feigning some sort of modest code of conduct to keep you interested, will find that their desire to get to who you really are wears thin when they learn that what they see is what they get, nothing more.

VIRGO AND ARIES

The fast and furious nature of Aries-born individuals irritates you in many ways, because they often don't appear to be thinking through their actions. You like to take your time to think things over at a slower pace to avoid errors of judgement. Aries is, by nature, very impulsive. However, if you happen to be a dynamic and speculative Virgo, you might like to take a chance with the Ram.

You might try your best to enamour Aries, but will think all the while that you are just not up to the task. And the Aries ego, without ever purposely trying to hurt you, may, at times, shock you, and give you good reason to believe they are deliberately trying to keep you down.

QUIZ:
HAVE YOU FOUND
YOUR PERFECT
MATCH?

Do you dare take the following quiz to see just how good a lover you are? Remember, although the truth sometimes hurts, it's the only way to develop your relationship skills.

We are all searching for our soulmate: that idyllic romantic partner who will fulfil our wildest dreams of love and emotional security. Unfortunately, finding true love isn't easy. Sometimes, even when you are in a relationship, you can't help but wonder whether or not your partner is right for you. How can you possibly know?

It's essential to question your relationships and to work on ways that will improve your communication and overall happiness with your partner. It's also a good idea, when meeting someone new, to study their intentions and read between the lines. In the first instance, when your hormones are taking over, it's easy to get carried away and forget some of the basic principles of what makes for a great relationship that is going to endure.

You're probably wondering where to start. Are you in a relationship currently? Are you looking for love, but finding it difficult to choose between two or more people? Are you simply not able to meet someone? Well, there are some basic questions you can ask yourself to discover the truth of just how well suited you and your partner are for each other. If you don't have a partner at the moment, you might like to reflect on your previous relationships to improve your chances next time round.

The following quiz is a serious attempt to take an honest look at yourself and see whether or not your relationships are on track. Don't rush through the questionnaire but think carefully about your practical day-to-day life and whether or not the relationship you are in genuinely fulfils your needs and the other person's needs. There's no point being in a relationship if you're gaining no satisfaction out of it.

Now, if you aren't completely satisfied with the results you get, don't give up! It's an opportunity for you to work at the relationship and to improve things. But you mustn't let your ego get in the road, because that's not going to get you anywhere.

Virgos are passionate and intense, even though their totem, the Virgin, seems to indicate otherwise. Therefore, you need love, affection, support and honesty. The ideal partner will be devoted to you, and never take your unconditional love for granted.

So here's a checklist for you, Virgo, to see if he or she's the right one for you.

Scoring System:

Yes = 1 point

No = 0 points

- ❓ Does he/she appreciate you for your mind as well as your body?

- ❓ Does he/she offer you passion and emotional comfort?

- ❓ Does he/she recognise that your selfless service is a blessing to them?

- ❓ Do they listen carefully when you need to be critical about something?

- ❓ Are they tidy and well groomed?

- ❓ Do they maintain a high standard of personal hygiene and cleanliness?

- ❓ Are they practical with money?

- ❓ Do they communicate their feelings to you?

- ❓ Do they respect your occasional need for solitude?

- ❓ Do they captivate your attention?

- ❓ Do they support your ideals as much as you do theirs?

- ❓ Do they express themselves easily, with a view to creating understanding?

❷ Do they have a systematic way of doing things that makes you feel in tune with them?

❷ Do they enjoy quiet moments with you in peaceful surroundings?

❷ Do they enjoy travelling and learning about the world?

❷ Do they devote time to spiritual or self-help practices?

Have you jotted down your answers honestly? If you're finding it hard to come up with the correct answers, let your intuition help and try not to force them. Of course, there's no point pretending and turning a blind eye to treatment that is less than acceptable, otherwise you're not going to have a realistic appraisal of your prospects with your current love interest. Here are the possible points you can score.

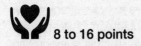 **8 to 16 points**

A good match. This shows you've obviously done something right, and that the partner you have understands you and is able to reciprocate in just the way you need. But this doesn't mean you should become lazy and not continue working on your relationship. There's always room to improve and make your already excellent relationship even better.

 5 to 7 points

Half-hearted prospect. You're going to need to work hard at your relationship, and this will require a close self-examination of just who may be at fault. You know, it takes two to tango and it's more than likely a combination of both your attitudes is what is dragging down your relationship. Systematically go over each of the above questions and try to make a list of where you can improve. I guarantee that your relationship will improve if given some time and sincerity on your part. If, after a genuine effort of working at it, you find things still haven't improved, it may be time for you to rethink your future with this person.

 0 to 4 points

On the rocks. I'm sorry to say that this relationship is not founded on a sufficiently strong enough base of mutual respect and understanding. It's likely that the two of you argue a lot, don't see eye to eye or, frankly, have completely different ideas of what sort of lifestyle and emotional needs you each have. The big question here is why are you still with this person?

Again, this requires some honest self-examination to see if there is some inherent insecurity which is causing you to hold on to something that has outgrown its use in your life. Old habits die hard, as they say, and you may also fear letting go of a relationship that you have become accustomed to, even though it doesn't fulfil your needs. Self-honesty is the key here. At certain times in life you may need to make some rather big sacrifices to move on to a new phase, which will then hopefully attract the right sort of partner to you.

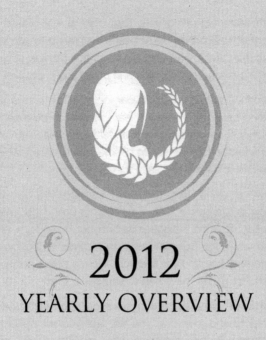

2012
YEARLY OVERVIEW

LIFE IS A TRAGEDY FOR THOSE WHO
FEEL, AND A COMEDY FOR THOSE
WHO THINK.

Jean de La Bruyére

❦ KEY EXPERIENCES ❧

With Mars activating your Sun sign at the outset of the year, you will be full of beans and raring to go. You must be careful, however, not to let this Martian energy dominate your relationships and make you impulsive.

Up until October, much of your focus will be on money, cutting back expenses and learning how to be a better fiscal manager. Saturn will certainly be teaching you some lessons about how to handle your finances, which appears to be the key issue for you this year.

However, don't worry too much, because you do have a few incidences of luck. From March until June, when Jupiter moves in the upper part of your horoscope, and then when the Sun activates your career prospects in June and July, you will find yourself in a better position, even though you have had to struggle a little.

With Saturn's transit through your zone of communication, contacts and journeys, you will find yourself seriously engaging in conversations and making deals, and probably travelling less than you would like. But this is important for you to solidify your position, clear your head and see exactly where you are going in the next twelve months.

With Mars transiting your zone of romance after the 11th of November, excellent romantic opportunities await you.

ROMANCE AND
FRIENDSHIP

It's a lucky year for you, Virgo, and that can be accounted for by Jupiter moving into one of the best positions of your horoscope for the first time in twelve years.

You are serious about love and romance this year, which is evidenced by Mars powerfully influencing your zone of marriage and relationships. But you may need to be careful that your desires and those of the ones you love don't come into conflict. Your willpower has been getting stronger than ever leading up to this year.

Your karmic planets influence both your career and home lives during 2012, so your relationships will hinge on finely balancing these areas. If you get the balance right, the rest will just fall into place.

The planet of love, Venus, makes its powerful influence felt in your life after the beginning of April. You can really strut your stuff on the world stage at that time, particularly in your work and social arenas. You will have a great deal of success, and your romantic aspirations can be fulfilled, especially after June.

You are extremely idealistic in your love life during the coming twelve months, as shown by Neptune, which recently entered your most important zone of personal and intimate relationships, including marriage.

You are committed to raising your standards, and finding the person who matches the dreams you have about love and commitment. But this year, you must also be careful not to allow your expectations to be unrealistic. If you raise the bar too high, mere mortals will be unable to meet your criteria.

 Relationships on the Rise

There are certain times of the year when planets support your romantic activities, and it's best to take full advantage of these dates to fully enjoy the opportunities that love has to offer.

The 4th of February is a key date, when Venus transits the zone of your horoscope that influences your sexual and intimate affairs. This should be a thoroughly enjoyable, physical period for you.

On March the 1st, and then again on April the 15th—but probably for this whole period—you will be particularly interested in developing a new friendship, or a relationship if you are still single. For those already committed, you may have some serious choices to make, especially if you have been in a relationship that is a little worn out.

Things could slow down a little after the 23rd of April, when Saturn casts its cautious eye on your social activities. You may want to enjoy things, but feel that someone is putting a dampener on the affair. You may need to step out of your social circle for a while.

ROMANCING AUGUST AND SEPTEMBER

Another couple of perfect opportunities to engage in romantic dalliances occur around the 18th of August and then again on the 29th of September. The Sun and Venus cast their attractive energies upon you and, in turn, you can cast your spell on potential partners.

You can increase your circle of friends after the 19th— you may need to stimulate your mind if you have been hanging out with the same people for too long.

November and December are key months, and around 18th of November you may be stimulated by a friend who dares you to try something different. That will lead to further sexual opportunities around the 13th of December. If that happens to involve a one-night stand, you may be surprised to find that by the 17th, you get a call back from that person, and a friendship may even develop into something a little more serious.

WORK AND MONEY

 Harness Your Moneymaking Powers

Making money can be summed up in an equation:

$$m\ (\$\ money) = e\ (energy) \times t\ (time) \times l\ (love)$$

If one of the above factors is not present—for example, energy or love—you could still make money, but you won't be ideally fulfilled in the process.

It's absolutely essential to understand the universal laws of attraction and success when speaking about money. It is also necessary to understand that, when you love what you do, you infuse your work with the qualities of attention, love and perfection.

With these qualities, you endow your work with a sort of electromagnetic appeal: a power that draws people to your work and causes them to appreciate what you do. This, in turn, generates a desire for people to use your services, buy your products and respect you for the great work you perform. This will without a doubt elevate you to higher and higher positions because you will be regarded as someone who exercises great diligence and skill in your actions.

As I continue to say, the one drawback in the first part of the year is the presence of Saturn in your zone of income. What this essentially means is that you may find it difficult to earn as much as you would like to, and all the way until August or early September, this frustration could build to a rather unmanageable level.

You need to contain this, and understand that your moneymaking powers are mostly influenced by your own thinking. You have to step out of your modest nature this year to try something bold, which is what Mars is hinting at by being associated with your Sun sign of Virgo.

In January and February, you must try to beautify your work. Pay some more attention to the presentation of material, even if what you do is simply crunching numbers. This will have a marked impact on those who look at your work, and they will be sufficiently impressed and possibly offer you some additional work, money or more interesting tasks.

JUPITER AND VENUS GET LUCKY

Jupiter and Venus are extremely lucky for you this year, particularly when they cross each other's paths throughout March, and continue to influence you throughout April. Thereafter, Venus is present in your career zone during May, providing you the opportunity to use your powers of persuasion or force someone's hand for a new position or pay rise. Don't be shy—ask for what you want.

Another hint I'm going to give you this year is to pay attention to how Neptune is influencing the area of your horoscope that involves public relations. You could be a little confused or inhibited by the fact that you are dealing with people in higher positions, whether in your workplace or in society.

Cast aside your fears, and boldly enter into negotiations and discussions with full confidence, forgetting about any class distinctions. When you meet your clients and business associates on the same level, you will be respected. And if you are respected, you have a better chance when asking for a higher fee or a better salary. Trust me.

In June and July, the upper part of your horoscope is fully activated, bringing with it extraordinary opportunities for work, self-esteem and moneymaking. For the first time this year, Mars exits your Sun sign in July and makes its entrance into your finance sector.

Notwithstanding the position of Saturn there as well, which slows things down, the Mars presence indicates that your drive to make things happen is likely to bring you greater income at this time. Don't let a few bumps stop you from achieving your goals, Virgo.

In August and September, you must take extra care not to spend too much money. Keeping up with the Joneses is a waste of time. With Mercury, the Sun and Venus all transiting your zone of expenses, you might forget that you will, at some stage, have to pay back the money on your credit cards. Try to stretch your dollar a little further, and you will be surprised at how making money becomes easier when you are saving more.

One of your luckiest planets, Venus, passes though your income zone in November, and then moves into your contracts sector in December. These are the periods when you will be able to tap into your moneymaking powers, and make the most of what life has to offer you, and continue right up to the end of 2012.

Tips for Financial Success

With your ability to make money this year, it will help to know when profits, income and business opportunities can augment your chances for putting more money in your bank.

Regarding profits, if you run an independent business you are likely to see an increase in turnover thanks to the influence of Venus around the 11th of January.

You need to watch your debts—which are influenced by the same planet—leading up to the 30th of March. Excessive expenditure could punch a hole in your bank account at this time.

Opportunities are plentiful, and Lady Luck blesses you around the 20th of April, when Jupiter is in an exact line with the Sun. With Saturn also influencing your zone of profits, there should be a steady flow of income at this time, especially around the 23rd of April.

After the 24th of May, Jupiter continues to throw luck your way with surplus cash. Remember, don't be too greedy, and put aside a little for a rainy day.

Your joint finances are highlighted around the 2nd of September, and this could result in some speculative investment after the 29th.

The eclipse of the 14th of November occurs in your zone of communications and contracts. Some important matters associated with your business will arise or some educational discussions will occur. You have the ability to see things more clearly when the hidden aspects of a situation emerge.

Between the 10th and the 25th of October, you should ask for a pay rise, and by the 18th of November, friendships and business interests could overlap nicely, creating some additional opportunities for more money.

Career Moves and Promotions

There is creative energy in the air, and when Mercury influences the zone of your horoscope that involves activity, fun and speculation, you will be full of ideas and ready to try something new. Actually, that could well be a thread throughout the whole of the year.

There are some key career dates throughout 2012, and the first of them is the 12th of February, when contractual opportunities and rapport with others give you the perfect combination of planetary energies with which make your move.

After the 22nd of May, Mercury influences your three zones of career, finance and workplace, and health. This hints at the fact that a career move now is opportune, but look after your physical wellbeing and don't overdo it. You may be burning the candle at both ends, and you're of no use to anyone if you're not in a good physical state.

Because you are notorious for being highly strung, due to the rulership of Mercury over your nervous system, this particular area of your body may need some vitamin supplements to keep you in tip-top condition.

NEGOTIATION TIME

On the 14th of September, and then again after the 2nd of October, your career planet, Mercury, provides you with a wonderful series of opportunities to change your work, ask for a promotion and even pursue an independent line of work.

Between the 18th of November and the 10th of December, be careful of committing to something that may not be what you expect. You have a feeling that something is not all it has been made out to be, and you should trust your feelings on the matter. You'll probably be proven correct.

 When to Avoid Office Politics

Office politics seem to be part and parcel of work these days, so it's good to know when antagonistic, stressful days are going to ruffle your feathers.

It's difficult when you are torn between two loyalties, particularly when they involve an ethical or moral viewpoint. If this is happening around you, you may have sleepless nights and be unable to come to a firm conclusion, especially if the problem is associated with friends. You could have some big decisions to make, and you have to rely on your higher self to help you with this.

After the 23rd of April, Saturn creates problems for you through secret enemies—people who oppose what you do and who you are—and you may need to prepare yourself for a difficult period.

However, Saturn cautions you to be calm and collected under the pressure. If you are able to use the power of this planet constructively and resist the temptation, it can be turned from a foe to a friend, and will work miraculously to help you win out against your competitors.

In fact, I was once given this piece of advice by an old white-haired astrologer in the south of India. Many of his predictions came true, and he mentioned the manner in which you can gently transform these Saturnine energies into fabulous luck.

However, your cool-headedness will not last because, after the 17th of August, Mars creates havoc in some area of your life or routine. This will, no doubt, cause problems for you up until the 1st of November. You will be hot-headed, irritable and argumentative. You may even do something so spontaneous that you regret it afterwards. Just think twice—even three times—before making a decision.

You have heightened career appetites towards the end of the year. As a result, after the 20th of December, you will find yourself at loggerheads with someone you work with or who has to serve you in some capacity.

HEALTH, BEAUTY AND LIFESTYLE

 Venus Calendar for Beauty

Most of us are under the misconception that Venus, the planet of love and beauty, relates only to our facial and bodily features. Well, this year Venus accentuates other aspects of your personality, such as your speech, especially after February the 26th, making you much more attractive by virtue of what you say.

Your health and beauty are also dependent on how healthy you are on the inside, and I can see that Venus brings with it some excellent paths towards wellbeing after the 6th of June, when it climbs your zone of health. At the same time, your diet and the type of lifestyle you are leading may come under some transformative influences, and that, too, will only help to enhance your looks, speech and general aura.

....

SLIM SATURN IN 2012

If you've been putting on the kilos recently, Saturn will help you this year by controlling your appetite. This will further enhance your looks and sense of wellbeing.

....

Venus affords you an incredible amount of luck, particularly in your workplace, after April, throughout May, and even into June, by making you adorable to your work colleagues and, more importantly, to your clients. This is where your good looks and charming personality will help you come out as a great success this year.

Throughout August and September, you can adopt some wonderful beauty ideas from friends, television shows and magazine articles, but you must be prepared to try a few things that may not be part of your usual beauty tools. Being experimental will not only create a new look for you, but will also give you the chance to break old habits in the way you view yourself.

Here is another well-guarded secret, dealing with developing a more elegant form of beauty based on your star sign and the transits of planets. Take advantage of those moments when rest, sleep and meditative rejuvenation allow you to revitalise yourself.

You can do this when, throughout the end of September and into October, you consider going on a retreat to pamper yourself with massages, healthy food and other spiritual techniques for rejuvenating your physical and emotional wellbeing. At this time, Venus will be transiting this quiet zone of your horoscope, and all of the above techniques will release powerful healing and beautifying energies within you.

 Showing off Your Virgo Traits

Each zodiac sign has its own unique power based on the elements and planets that rule it. Unfortunately, most people don't know how to tap into this power and bring out their greatest potential to achieve success in life.

What are some of the positive traits you possess, Virgo? And how can you make them work for you in the coming twelve months?

This year, for the first time in twelve long years, the excellent and lucky planet Jupiter is creating a favourable aspect to those born under the sign of Virgo. In other words, your Virgo Sun will be accentuated by the beneficial rays of jovial Jupiter.

....

JOVIAL JUPITER

Jupiter brings an inner sense of confidence, luck and unexpected opportunities that allows you to showcase your wonderful Virgo traits of service, communication and tender care for those you love. In your workplace in particular, these traits will be noted by the people who matter most.

....

Patience is one of your most excellent personality traits, and you will need it in full measure throughout August, with Mars and Saturn influencing your zone of income.

Mercury and the Sun will be in the hidden zone of your horoscope in August, indicating that you will be able to use your deeper powers of analysis and observation to steer yourself though this tough time. Yet again, this is precisely how you can make the most of your star sign traits and not be overwhelmed by the peaks and troughs that life brings.

September is a wonderful time, when your ruling planet, Mercury, returns to your Sun sign, underpining your feeling of mirth, joy and confidence in relationships. You will be feeling young, happy and very playful indeed as a result of your ruler coming back to play with you.

It's all systems go after October, when shadowy circumstances surrounding your work clear up, giving you the best possible chance of furthering your career. Along with Venus moving through your Sun sign in October, and then through your finance zone in November, the last part of the year shows that you are able to capitalise on your best traits, and even get some extra cash in your pocket as a result.

Best Ways to Celebrate

When you celebrate your birthday, anniversary and other important events, it's important for friends and loved ones to understand that the Virgo temperament is not always excited about surprises, especially when too many people could possibly embarrass them.

This is an unusual year for you, because ordinarily I would say to follow the line of least resistance and use your ruling planet, Mercury, to determine the sorts of things, places and types of people you should celebrate with to enjoy yourself to the maximum.

This year, however, your horoscope is dominated by Mars, and its presence in your Sun sign at the outset shows you have much more of a physical appetite than usual, which will most certainly colour the way you want to enjoy yourself and celebrate throughout the year.

This may sound strange, but, especially in the first couple of months of the year, you may simply want to celebrate by spending time alone in your most comfortable jeans or track pants, turning the music up loud, and dancing till you drop. Nothing wrong with that!

Jupiter has a spiritual connotation, so it's quite likely, while it moves across the upper zone of your horoscope, all the way through to June, that spiritual activities like meditation and yoga (which also allow Mars to get your body involved in spiritual practices) will let you to combine spirituality with physicality to have a really great time and get fit at the same time.

POWER OF JUPITER

Yes, this year does seem to be all about celebrating life—not just your birthday or special events that come around from time to time, but beyond those limited forms of enjoyment, use the power of Jupiter to enjoy each moment as it arises.

Celebrations are most definitely in order when Jupiter and Venus combine in your zone of career after the end of June and into July. You may acquire a new job or assume a new post, and then, during Venus's transit of your zone of profits in August and September, the planets once again indicate earnings from additional money. Good for you. Keep thinking positive thoughts to attract good events into your life.

KARMA, SPIRITUALITY AND EMOTIONAL BALANCE

The principal planets governing your spirituality are Saturn and Venus. Jupiter, the natural leader of spiritual matters, happens to be in your zone of spirituality throughout a large part of the year, and therefore 2012 will not be a year where you have to make too much effort to experience the inner worlds.

Philosophy, learning new languages, investigating the law and other highly intellectual (as well as spiritual) pursuits will be high on your agenda, especially throughout the period of January to June.

When Jupiter and Venus conjoin in the latter part of March, some good fortune based on past karma will bring you a pleasant surprise.

Important dates for performing good deeds for others, and for allowing your compassionate nature to shine through, include the 4th of February and the 1st of March. On this latter date, you may have to look after a child or give up some of your past conditioned ideas to get with the program in the present world climate.

There are a few other key dates, including the 29th of September, when Venus once again brings you very powerful influences of a spiritual nature. These can trigger some deep inner understanding and personal transformations in your life.

However, there's no point gaining all this spiritual knowledge if you can't apply it on a practical level. Therefore, during the second half of November, especially around the 18th and beyond, you will be in a position to test your inner knowledge, and see how practical you need to be, especially if you are in a marriage or close personal relationship. The concept of unconditional love will be very much highlighted during this phase.

PSYCHIC INSIGHTS

You can experience clairvoyant, clairaudient, and even clairsentient insights, which relate to the inner eye, the inner ear, and the inner sense of touch. Basically, you are connected to people and the spiritual dimensions during the last couple of months of 2012.

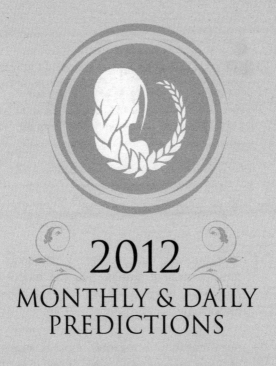

2012
MONTHLY & DAILY
PREDICTIONS

AFTER THE GAME, THE KING AND
THE PAWN GO INTO THE SAME BOX.

Italian proverb

☙ JANUARY ☙

Monthly Highlight

Don't let the Sun and Pluto cause you to play power games with the ones you love. Be persuasive but not dominating in the way you handle lovers and children.

Work could be confusing this month but there will also be moments of great satisfaction.

1 Your business matters seem to be under a fortunate star at present. You can expect to make some real progress materially, socially and intellectually.

2 You'll come to a decision about a lingering business issue or some family friction today. It's imperative that you don't dredge up old stories. Leave them in the past.

3 An occasional disapproving word from someone is nothing to be too disheartened about. If this person insists on snapping at you, however, then it's high time you spoke up yourself.

4 Don't deny the spontaneity in your personality today. You might be too absorbed in doing a job correctly, forgetting the greater power of who you *are*. Remain aware.

5 Recent confusion in your relationships gives way to an enlightened view of a current association. Your perspective was skewed by your rose-coloured glasses.

6 You can either get caught up in the same old rigmarole with family members, or try a different approach today. A bit of reverse psychology goes a long way!

7 It's almost certain you'll take on board a position that will up the ante on your weekly income and add prestige to your daily life.

8 You'll be tempted to dive into a business deal or residential offer that could put you behind the eight ball financially if you don't read the small print.

9 After all this time, you still find the same feelings arising in association with a certain situation. It's time you reassessed where you're going with this.

10 You might decide to become a recluse, shunning contact with others for a while. Your new values are an orderly existence along with neatness and organisation.

11 Take some time out to listen to conventional wisdom today, because you may be reckless and fiery. Practical advice may help you channel productive pursuits.

12 There's the prospect of an exciting and nicely challenging day today, but only if you make an effort to clean up that backlog of work!

13 Don't get carried away with bits and pieces that have no connection to the greater scheme of things. Delegate the small stuff so your single focus is the big picture!

14 If you're home or job hunting, today is the day when you could find success in the form of an offer or referral. Settle for no less than what you believe is fair!

15 Take advantage of the great influences coming your way over the next 24 hours. Unhappy family situations will reach a turning point, and you're the meat in the sandwich.

16 You won't be satisfied until you have the biggest and best of anything in your path today. Everything will be done in a big way, so you'll be spreading yourself thinly.

17 Today, you can channel your moods and energy into providing useful suggestions to loved ones. Do this subtly, and you will gain some benefits in a roundabout way.

18 Sometimes you have to boil down the sap to get to the syrup. Look a little more deeply to see the true worth of a special person you met recently. Don't take things at face value for the time being. Wait.

19 The planets are influencing your professional destiny at the moment. Luckily, your grievance and doubt over a work matter is short lived.

20 You may feel as though you're being ignored by the people closest to you, but you probably haven't noticed they have issues, too. Try to be more compassionate just now.

21 You may invite trouble today in your family circle by not agreeing with a 'good' idea. You're bored with tradition, so do your own thing and avoid the hassle.

22 You're action-oriented today, and want to be the centre of all activity. Because of all of the extravagance, this period may trouble you with excessive debt.

23 You will go out of your way to impress others with your influence or wealth in an attempt to appear important. However, all that glitters is not gold.

24 Matters of cleanliness and sterile environments are important today. You're trying to rediscover parts of yourself that are hidden. This is the right time to do it.

25 You may use your abilities to uncover corruption today, or find greater compassion for people who have been victims of the abuses of the world or in your workplace.

26 Your thinking may be messed up and uncertain at the moment. Nervous exhaustion could occur. If you enjoy writing, you can find inspiration in it at this time, and it will clear your mind as well.

27 Just now you stand a very good chance of being used, deceived or taken advantage of in some way. This is a wonderful time to figure out who your true friends and admirers are.

28 According to some people, you're not to blame—so you shouldn't beat yourself up about it! Your inner self tells you they made their choices, just as you did, so rise above the idea of victimhood.

29 Refrain from talking at people during any meetings. You want things to work out as you've imagined them, so do your best to say things with a smile on your face.

30 It's an excellent day to make changes to your routine. Find out what's necessary for your long-term goals, as these plans are going to be your future foundations.

31 It's pointless making out you know what is going on when those who love you know you have little idea! Embrace what's new, and be gentle on yourself.

❄ FEBRUARY ❄

 Monthly Highlight

Your work is coloured by emotionalism, and you could be in two minds about how you want to proceed this month.

Money matters are a concern, with Saturn making it difficult for you to move forward financially. Neptune, the Sun and Mercury also indicate considerable debt if you are not careful.

Venus is in a perfect position to enhance your relationships, but you may be pushing too hard, particularly after the 22nd. Just relax and enjoy them.

1 Discussions about work are high on your agenda just now, but you may be over-reactive to others' responses to your suggestions. It's early days, so don't take no as really meaning no just yet.

2 Family members disapprove of what you're doing in your work or your social life. This could create problems for you, but why not draw a line in the sand and live life on your own terms?

3 You are likely to be angry today, and the Moon and Mars combination makes you trigger happy. You need to employ diplomatic means to resolve your problems.

4 'Who rules the roost?' will be an important question in your social affairs today. Ego or power plays make things uncomfortable in your usual peer group.

5 Surround yourself with people who've experienced similar things to you. You can gain an all-round understanding as well as approval, provided you're prepared to accept your faults.

6 You may be afraid of pooling your resources and physical energies with someone, because you may not gain the recognition you desire. Today is a day of spiritual trust.

7 Today's a full Moon and you'll achieve a lot, but not if you're liasing with other people on your tasks. They could hinder rather than help you.

8 There's an upswing in your romantic desires at present, and the Moon and Mars in combination make you impulsive and quite sexual. It could be quite a fun day.

9   You continue to be playful, and want to explore what's on offer in your personal relationships. However, you may need to break some boundaries.

10 If you're in a business relationship, you may have to decide whether your partner has the same goals as you. You could be distracted and starting to wonder whether the grass is greener on the other side.

11 You're changing your patterns of thinking regarding money at the moment, and this is a good thing. Curtailing extraneous expenditure will help you save money.

12 If ex-lovers are trying to make a comeback in your life, this could throw you off-kilter. You need to think carefully about re-engaging with people who've done the dirty on you in the past.

13 A chance meeting with an old friend is likely around this time, but you may realise that you're now completely different people. How things change! Such is life.

14 Unresolved issues with a relative or friend may cause you to travel and be inconvenienced as a result. It's probably better to deal with this issue via the telephone.

15 Bury the hatchet now if there are problems on the home front. It's time to move on and remove those negative feelings.

16 Hanging on to the residence you live in is part of an emotional hang-up. You need to make a clean break, and enjoy some new and exciting exploits in life. Don't fear about making a change.

17 Love and relationships are playing on your mind. You're wondering whether to force someone's hand in a situation where you're not clear on what they want. There's no harm in giving it a little push.

18 If you're hurt and confused by a relationship, it's important to remind yourself that time heals all wounds. Trust in this healing process.

19 There's some confusion about current workplace issues, due to Neptune. You need to be creative and imaginative in the way you deal with obstructive individuals.

20 You need to step up your exercise regime. You're probably feeling sedentary right now, and need to get that blood of yours pumping. Head out and clear your mind.

21 The new Moon means both the Sun and the Moon occupy your relationship sphere. It's time to clear up any misunderstandings or, better still, start a new relationship. This is an excellent omen for satisfaction.

22 A change is as good as a holiday, as they say. If you're not happy with your existing clientele or friends, venture forth and seek out new people.

23 If your partner has a personal problem, make sure you take the time to listen to their grievance. Today's theme is unconditional love, which means you may have to put your own stuff on hold.

24 You need to empower others as well as yourself today. By helping those around you, they will in turn help you. You need to see the bigger picture in your relationships, as well as in your professional life.

25 If some of your closest friends don't seem to be open and honest with you, you need to try different strategies to raise their standards of integrity. Here's a suggestion: straightforwardness.

26 You need to handle the details of a financial transaction yourself, rather than trusting someone else. If there is an element of mistrust hanging around now, why not do things yourself?

27 If you take other people's statements too personally, you're doomed to be upset by your relationships. Don't assume people are levelling their remarks only at you today.

28 Higher education activities are part of your current cycle. Expanding your knowledge and learning more about many different things will interest you.

29 The month finishes on a professional note. You feel as though you have some good luck, but you shouldn't let that deter you from making your best efforts.

✿ MARCH ✿

Monthly Highlight

After the 1st, Venus triggers your desire to travel. Your itchy feet will certainly find you moving about, and even planning an overseas trip. The Sun transiting your zone of shared resources after the 16th indicates a greater focus on shared money.

1 It's quite alright to be indecisive, as long as you're not going to procrastinate too long. A decision relating to work may bother you today.

2 Show off your best talents to your friends without fear of reprisal. Don't be scared that you may outshine someone today. It's all about being recognised.

3 You can dance on the romantic stage of life and attract a lot of new friends just now. There is the possibility of developing a friendship into a more serious affair.

4 There's a strong cultural vibe around you, and you may take an interest in foreign issues, cuisine and people who don't come from where you do.

5 If you're hiding your talents, it will be pretty hard for you to withhold them at the moment. You may need to spend a little time honing your skills and abilities, but some discipline will be worth it in the long run, too.

6 Don't let fear cripple you. If you have worries about your health or that of someone else, the quickest way to resolve them is to get an expert opinion. It's probably nothing.

7 Your energy is on the increase. However, you may feel self-conscious about doing something and the opinions of others. Do what makes you feel good.

8 Reassess the work you do against who you are and where your true talents lie. You may be trying to slot into a type of job that's not exactly the best choice.

9 Mars will provoke you and your partners (both personal and professional) into thrashing out the details of finances. Your value system may be at odds with someone else's.

10 You could be treading on eggshells to keep the peace, especially if you're married. Harmony, of course, is essential, but not at the expense of your self-esteem.

11 Deliberate carefully before passing judgement on a current issue. A serious conversation will go better if you have your facts at hand.

12 You could be investing more time than is necessary on the tasks that are expected of you. Jupiter makes it easy to get your schedule in order, so why not use these energies wisely? Break things down into their constituent parts and prioritise.

13 Home is where the heart is. If you aren't in the place you'd like to be, try enjoying what you *have* and stop focusing on what you *don't*!

14 Venus is prodding you to travel right now, so it's not a bad idea to get away, to explore the hidden side of your personality and that of your closest mate.

15 You can't ignore your physical needs, with Mercury hinting at the fact that you'll be interested in developing your physical as well as emotional needs at the moment. There's a playful energy associated with this planet.

16 It's all about entertainment at present. If you've been burning the candle at both ends with work, work, and more work, it's time to let your hair down and relax.

17 'Which romantic cherry should you pick from the tree of love?' is the question for some Virgos just now. There's a challenge in knowing how to sort the men from the boys, so to speak.

18 The presence of hardworking Saturn doesn't mean that you should have to endure a hard slog all the time. A clever approach to tasks means that working smart can yield good results, which is probably better than the original angle.

19 You have an endless supply of energy for work projects just now, but your health could suffer as a result. Moderate your timetable so you can enjoy other things in life.

20 You're confused over your partner—probably their health or their financial situation. With the Sun influencing them at the moment, you're probably over-reacting.

21 You can strike a deal right now with a high-powered individual. This person can open a few doors for you and make your work much more worthwhile.

22 You'll be one of the quickest sprinters off the block in trying to analyse yourself and others. Some of your assessments will be correct, and you'll be in a better position to deal with your relationships as a result.

23 A slower, steadier approach seems to be the key today. Others may be hurrying you or reaching their objectives more quickly, but your determined and efficient work will win out.

24 You could become concerned if your employer hands you a new set of instructions with fine print attached. Mistrust could cloud your judgement, but take this as simply being all in a day's work.

25 Mental discipline and a greater degree of concentration may be momentarily difficult, but will be important in maintaining your professionalism. Don't allow others to distract you.

26 You will continue to rush around madly and possibly not finish the tasks you're supposed to. You're partly to blame for this, but there are other factors, too. At least take responsibility for your part.

27 You could be lucky just now, but be careful not to lunge at an opportunity too quickly. A relaxed and poised attitude will make a greater impression on others.

28 You may need to take control of a situation if management appears to be out to lunch. This may be a daunting task, but it will reveal some of your hidden talents.

29 Your progressive methods may be out of step with your peers at the moment. It's best not to talk about what you're doing but let the results speak for themselves.

30 You need to define your relationships more clearly, especially those of a social nature. You needn't take any heat from those who are pressuring you to be different. Be true to yourself today.

31 A team effort is what's needed if you're working collaboratively on some ideas. Being an island unto yourself will only alienate you from your friends and their help.

❧ APRIL ❧

 Monthly Highlight

Legal matters and issues related to education aggravate you. Your main attention may be on your travel plans, which are highlighted this month.

Saturn briefly touches your zone of communication, which could make your discussions a little more sombre and serious than usual.

---

1 You could feel somewhat alone today when looking at your future. Even if you're married or in a committed relationship, you might feel as though you're treading the path by yourself. Sometimes that's necessary to achieve success, after which you can share the spoils.

---

2 You're probably your own worst enemy today, because you're looking at the situation from the wrong perspective. Put a positive spin on yourself just now.

---

3 Don't leave anything to chance. Manage your personal affairs as efficiently as possible. Remain beyond reproach.

---

4 Clarity is necessary in your relationships because Mercury is retrograde. Seek more information from your partner or friend so that you can make a correct assessment. Don't jump to conclusions.

5 You need to manage your time as effectively as possible. Financial matters could drain you of a lot of creative energy. The sooner you get them out of the way, the better.

6 The full Moon accentuates your focus on money, material goods and finance. An issue relating to your income could finally become clear.

7 Communication with your work colleagues requires you to set your goals together. Find the common thread, and your power as a unit will be greatly enhanced.

8 A stroke of luck could land you a better job, or at least a better position within your current organisation. Effectively improving your communication is at the heart of this.

9 Friends are accommodating just now, and could be willing to visit you for a change, rather than vice versa. It's nice to see others making an effort, isn't it?

10 Venus gives you extraordinary charm and luck at the moment. Just don't blow it by spending too much time on social concerns rather than business responsibilities.

11 Take a risk today and ask for what you want. Chances are you'll shock your employer into giving it to you.

12 At present, you have a competitive spirit, but you must learn to be a good sport as well. You're not always going to win, but it's the development of your skills and the fun you have that counts.

13 You feel reasonably happy in the role you're playing professionally at the moment, but you may need to spend some money to improve your skills.

14 Expenses could spiral out of control through a false sense of security. Don't be scared to create a budget for yourself.

15 Continue to manage your savings and monitor your spending. Have a plan for your future security. Something may be amiss in your superannuation arrangement.

16 You feel idealistic about your relationships today, but could be let down if you're not getting as much as you give. Why not try a new strategy?

17 Before agreeing to a course of action, think carefully. Your impulse may be based on the fact that you want to be acknowledged or loved. It could backfire.

18 Please note that real estate matters will work well for you only if you've done your homework on the banking, interest and other important aspects of finance. Talk to your bank manager.

19 You are erratic and could make decisions that are not based in rational thinking. Dreams are fine, but if they have no basis in reality, the end result is zero. Keep it real.

20 You may not understand where all your money is going at present. It may have something to do with your children or your partner. You need to extend your budget to include them as well.

21 There's nothing like the present to invest additional time in yourself. Jupiter's movement through your spiritual sector tells me that you need a deeper analysis of yourself to gain a better understanding.

22 You need self-imposed simplicity to streamline your day-to-day activities just now. Stop trying to complicate your life and your work.

23 News may come of an annual event at which your attendance is compulsory. You need to tailor your affairs to fit in with this slight imposition.

24 You could do with some advice from an experienced professional at the moment. You may be unclear about the best way to climb the ladder of success.

25 Democratic processes don't always work, and you feel like smashing through some of the obstacles that are stopping you from fulfilling yourself creatively. You must be intent, but also adhere to the proper course of action.

26 You can expect some surprising luck from an unusual avenue. Still, give it the acid test before agreeing.

27 Someone's unseen hurt could be affecting their behaviour. Look beneath the surface to find the truth.

28 Unexpected twists or changes in your routine will cause you problems. Remind yourself that what's outside the agreed scope should not be considered.

29 Sometimes even the most magnificent plans can't stop a day being ruined. It's quite probable that a sudden change of opinion by someone could do just that.

30 Balance your work and play to create the best opportunities for yourself. Scattering your energies is illogical, so it's best to collect yourself rather than doing too much.

❧ MAY ❧

Monthly Highlight

You could be confused about relationships, especially in the first week of the month, due to the influence of Neptune and Mars. Don't try to force them, and allow the relationships to tell you where they should be going.

Social opportunities through work present you with a chance for change. The Sun and Jupiter are lucky for you in the zone of past karma. This could indeed be a lucky month for you, Virgo.

---

1 You're inclined to do some number crunching today. Go through your contracts and paperwork associated with finances. Avoid impulses.

---

2 You'll be feeling diplomatic just now, but don't rush into anything for which you haven't yet built safeguards. You make the decision, even if someone else is convincing you to do otherwise.

---

3 There's no substitute for good, healthy food to bring you satisfying results, health-wise. Rest is also necessary now.

---

4   If you're charged with incompetence, you'll be angry for a while, but the best thing to do is simply keep your receipts and a level head. These will be ample proof to support your case.

5   You'll be nervous about speaking to a group or a crowd, but if you refuse, they could take it as an insult. You can't neglect your responsibilities in this respect.

6   It's a full Moon and you mustn't let fleeting doubt undermine your true feelings about the path you've chosen in life. The attitude of gratitude is important today.

7   You need to incorporate a certain amount of dictatorial style today, to have the psychological edge over your competitors or, for that matter, those closest to you.

8   You need to get back that feeling you had when you were first attracted to the one you love. Why not try some uncommon methods to revitalise the relationship?

9   You might be feeling just that little bit crazy today, especially if you're surrounded by resistant nuts who don't want to be constructive in working with you. Did you know nuts are there to be crushed?

10 You need a visual kit by your side at the moment. The visuals will help you accomplish your tasks and, if necessary, explain what you want to others.

11 Dynamic partnerships and negotiations are on the cards today. However, you need to scrap your previous series of ideas and start afresh.

12 If you need to split from someone in a social sense, consider this an insignificant bump in the road of your life. New connections are going to be made. Don't worry.

13 Random events—or incidents of coincidence, as I call them—are the things that life is made of. Don't dismiss insignificant events as unimportant. Something big is mounting.

14 Someone offers you a vague and broad idea of what they want, but it's hard for you to put your finger on exactly what that is. It will be necessary for you to lay down a bedrock of clarity before agreeing to anything.

15 Your past actions are now coming to fruition and new opportunities are going to appear magically on your doorstep. An emergency may, however, hold things up for a little while.

16 Your bin is stuffed with so much useless information that you need a spring clean and you need it now. This will create the space to bring in bigger and better things.

17 If you're feeling drained in your work, it's because you haven't tracked your business and personal affairs adequately. Take stock of your life so that you have greater control.

18 Someone's cooked up a report that may not be true, and you have to go through the tedious exercise of proving why it's false. However, your hard work will pay off.

19 If you get wind of a vacancy in a professional capacity, you must unabashedly take advantage of the opportunity. Your luck continues just now.

20 If you contradict your superiors at the moment, it may only serve to prove your ignorance in some matter. You need to withhold information until you are clear on the bigger picture.

21 You could be tense and frantic when it's not necessary just now. You don't need to make too much effort to get what you want financially or romantically today.

22 There may be a fascinating shift in your work, even though it's rather puzzling to you. Go with the flow, and explore what's on offer, even if it seems a little strange.

23 Your attention is on a friend today, but theirs could be elsewhere. Don't magnify any imagined excuses for this—there is probably a legitimate reason why they are being so distant.

24 People may seem moderately amused at what you choose for your attire today, but at least you'll be original.

25 A hated counterpart may be trying to stir you up. The onus is on you not to play into that. Ignore them—they're probably just an idiot.

26 You need to get rid of your dogmatic viewpoints, because they are only going to cause problems between you and someone you genuinely like. Don't let religious or political differences get in the way of a good relationship.

27 You may need to help someone who's having some physical or mental trouble at the moment. They will come out of this unscathed.

28 Any bigotry on your part will undermine your good attempts today. Try to step aside from any sort of racism—or philosophical or religious differences—to be successful just now.

29 Someone could misrepresent themselves and you'll strangely believe them. You need to scrutinise people before saying yes, even if they seem like nice enough characters.

30 A collapsed romance is not the end of the world, unless, of course, you've been silly enough to loan someone money in the process. Keep business and pleasure distinctly separate.

31 You may have to modify your opinion on something, and that could impact on a friend. Minimise your guilt about this, because you know your decision is based on truth.

❧ JUNE ❧

 Monthly Highlight

You are full of energy this month. Especially after the 8th, the combination of Mars and the Sun indicate that you want to be physical, to exercise and to feel youthful strength. That's fine, as long as you don't steamroll others in the process.

Finances improve after the 16th, but you may end up spending more than you would like to after the 25th.

---

1 You want to come out the winner, but you'll have to restrain yourself if you're contesting a certain dragon on the work front. Remain co-operative, and remember that you don't need to go into battle.

---

2 You need to simplify your theories to make them understandable to underlings who aren't as clever as you. That will be your challenge today.

---

3 If you must manipulate a situation, at least do it with honesty. That way you can create the opportunities you know you want, without any hindrance from family members.

---

4 Keep your meetings a little more informal today if you wish to make an impression. Because of this, your business activities should go well.

5 Don't blow a romantic opportunity for the sake of being overly sentimental and emotional. Balance your emotions with some intellect today.

6 If you're sitting in on a meeting that may decide your future financial or professional life, remember that it's not always about what you do, but who you are that counts.

7 There's an important development in your workplace occurring at the moment. You could have a breakthrough in your systems or methods, and this is going to streamline your work and save you time.

8 Your high-energy work levels might clash with family engagements or commitments. Someone on the home front may be pressuring you about this at the moment.

9 Plan your tasks carefully, get it out of the way, and then spend some time helping your partner with their workload. This will help cement the bonds of love between you.

10 You don't have to be angry, but you could be quietly assertive in demanding that some of your needs be met. The person you love could be holding out on you just now.

11 You don't believe a story that's been told to you recently and you need much more convincing. But are you looking at the negatives again, rather than the positives?

12 You need to keep your feelings to yourself, especially if you have doubts about the truth of some gossip going around. This will be even more difficult, however, if the gossip is about you know who—yes, you.

13 You need to keep those you love onside. Know on which side your bread is buttered at the moment.

14 You'll have to put aside your mistrust of someone when their calls for help result in your kind-hearted nature coming to the fore. Rendering assistance will resolve a past issue today.

15 Self-sacrifice continues to be a key word for you over these next few days. As long as you don't begrudge the help you give others, the resulting karma will be good. You may not see it immediately, but it will come back to you.

16   There's no point getting angry if someone changes their mind just now. You need to discipline yourself, and take full control of your own energies, because there's no way you're going to control theirs.

17   You may have had your heart set on an important business meeting or dinner engagement that might not come to pass, but the reason for this will become clearer as the day moves forward.

18   Today, you'll learn some new lessons that will help you in a variety of areas in your life. The information may come through a work colleague, who is welcome just now.

19   You may be putting people on pedestals for a number of reasons, but importantly, this could have something to do with the fact you're not yet realising your own greatness. Why not focus a little on that for a while?

20   It's a new Moon in your zone of friendships. Welcome new friends and acquaintances, and extend yourself in the way you view others.

21   A friend who's not yet paid you back from the last round of help may impose on you again. You have to be cruel to be kind and say no this time.

22 You're probably tired of helping everyone only to feel that no one's reciprocating. You mustn't impose on others, but if they're not forthcoming with their help, you may need to demand it...in a nice way.

23 Time alone will give you a boost mentally, but don't forget to reach out to others and share the wealth of knowledge you're acquiring at the moment.

24 A sibling or close relative could be in some sort of strife. However, you mustn't become embroiled in their problems, as much as you want to help them.

25 You could have a problem recalling an important piece of information that someone's been waiting for. You might have to admit you're at fault and let them throw their hissy fit.

26 Don't get involved in speculative financial schemes. It's unlikely that a quick fix will make you rich. It's only the very occasional lucky winner who can boast of gaining millions in a split second. Continue to work hard.

27 Those you socialise with could end up stepping away from you if you get too serious about your version of the truth. Go slowly.

28 Stop being so wasteful with your energy. Resist pursuing everyone for fear of being alone. Let your energies and magnetic powers draw the right people into your life just now.

29 Your personal views mustn't get mixed up with your professional duties. You may need to hold back from speaking your mind on something, as much as you want to voice your opinion.

30 An opportunity to materialise a desire relating to property or a vehicle could eventuate today. Purchasing a car could be on the cards.

JULY

 Monthly Highlight

This is a quiet time of year, with the Sun transiting your zone of secrets. Charitable work, spiritual energies and other meditative insights will come to you now. It's a good time to sleep a little bit more as well.

1 It's a lucky month, with Venus and Jupiter in your work zone. However, your emotions are drawn to other matters. Focus on the things that count.

2 Don't be too flamboyant about the way you present yourself. Your image could be more important than you think.

3 A love affair could be ready to blossom, but you may jeopardise that by nitpicking and criticising the person in question. Try to be gracious to them, even if there are glaring mistakes being made on their part.

4 Romance is enticing you to forget everything else and spend time with a special person just now. It could mean putting aside work and social commitments to investigate this potential relationship more thoroughly.

5 Your creative energies are soaring at present, and you can use them in many areas of your life. An unexpected romantic doorway to your future is likely to be opened.

6 Stop hiding your talents—it's not advisable if you want people to recognise you. Fortune awaits, but you have to be bold and prepared to show others who you are.

7 Something's not right in your marriage or relationship, and there's some confusion over how you should approach your partner. Can I recommend one word? *Honesty*.

8 You mustn't let the rust set in on your relationships, or it will be extremely difficult to get those cogs moving again. Try some WD-40 of understanding and compassion to lubricate the relationship and get things back on track.

9 An unexpected event relating to finances could rock you to the core. But this will only happen if you haven't put in place measures to protect your savings and income. Look at insurance.

10 An argument over money is looming. Don't get sucked into the blame game. Be accountable for your expenditure, and accept where you've been wrong. This is the way towards reconciliation.

11 Things are actually stable, contrary to what others may want you to believe. You must trust your own assessment of things, rather than getting upset by what other people say.

12 Buying the latest kitchen, dashing off to the shops and recklessly spending money means you're operating on impulses. Plan a little, and look around a bit more.

13 You need to become a little more hip—a little more conversant with the younger folk—to keep up with what's happening in their world. This will be hard if you're used to your own ways. Open your mind a little today.

14 Moderation should be one of your key words at the moment, especially if the Moon makes you feel more emotional. Conserving your resources and energies is vital just now.

15 You could go against academic consensus; the group is not always right. The atmosphere may be extreme if you break ranks, but you need others to acknowledge that you're not a pushover.

16 It could be a rather difficult day, one where the demands of your profession and your employers start to take a toll on your wellbeing. Maybe you could do with a day off?

17 Take control of the situation if you have to. If that's not going to work, you may need to step away. They say that too many cooks spoil the broth, which is the case in your current social clique.

18 You need to regroup your ideas and make some changes to get yourself back on track. Someone you know may have parallel issues, so you can talk about these things.

19 You need to give yourself adequate personal space and some me time in the next couple of days. Your judgement may otherwise become impaired. Resist calls to socialise for a while.

20 To improve skill, you need to work at that task repetitively. In other words, practice makes perfect. If something is baffling your outlook, this is the only way to get it right.

21 The priorities you've set may be unconvincing to others just now. You may have to develop greater communication between you to get them onside.

22 Although there's a stack of new friends coming your way, some unseen boredom could be a shock to your system. Have a Plan B ready, just in case.

23 Your personal organiser could be loaded with meetings, but many of them seem to relate to paying bills, or getting financial or legal advice. Put a few social activities in there as well.

24 Conveying an idea may simply be a matter of changing the terminology. The venture you're discussing may depend on it. A new chapter is about to flip open. Are you ready for it?

25 Your silence is the best poison against a vehement peer. You need to maximise your leverage using the knife of logic. You don't have to broadcast your disapproval.

26 If you trace where you are in your life right now, you'll see that it has to do with the choices you've made. Don't blame your troubles on life, but take full responsibility for them. Your diet should consist mainly of faith tablets today.

27 Don't be gullible and believe everyone at the moment, especially if the subject relates to tax and finance. If the newsreaders are showering muck all over you, clean it up with your own discrimination.

28 You can't defeat others by playing your principles against theirs. If you're dealing with family members, be determined to withhold information rather than try to convert them.

29 If you can't fix the defects in others, leave them alone and lead by example. This is the only thorough antidote.

30 One of your enterprises—a creative one—may start to roll forward. The season is right, and you'll have sufficient support from others to make this happen.

31 Record your ideas to get some sort of orderliness going now. Keep a small notepad handy, and jot down your ideas as and when they arise. It sounds strange right now, but compiling your thoughts will pay off eventually.

AUGUST

 Monthly Highlight

This is a social period, with Venus moving into your zone of friendships and social activities. This is a month when you may find yourself in the company of beautiful people or feel beautiful yourself.

Be careful not to travel compulsively, because you might later realise it was a mistake.

---

1 You mustn't let your ambitions get in the way of expressing your feelings to loved ones, because you may be so busy today that you overlook their needs. Give your loved ones some attention, too.

---

2 Counselling others may take up quite a bit of time, but in the end it will benefit you as well. It is worthwhile helping those who, in turn, are going to serve you in some capacity. Put aside the time, even if it's slightly irritating.

---

3 An unexpected opportunity may mean you have to travel. Weighing up the pros and cons, however, will put you back on track.

4   You're finding new ways to deal with people in order to achieve your professional ambitions. You'll be stepping outside the box to try a few different things. They will work.

5   An institution you may be dealing with, probably in the financial or banking arena, may be restricting you. As well as being frustrating, it can also put your plans on hold. Just remember, none of these problems are lasting, they're just temporary hurdles to overcome.

6   You have to re-route your disciplinary instincts today to have some fun. Change your routine for a day or so, because it will give you the opportunity to see things from a different perspective.

7   You may be feeling somewhat isolated right now, but that's just because the universe requires you to spend some time alone to readjust and reassimilate.

8   You have to aspire to unusual things today. If boredom is setting in, try something different to lighten your load.

9 This is a reflective day, even though you see busy times ahead. Mustering up the strength and clarity, along with a plan to achieve your goals, is important at times like this.

10 You need to get plenty of rest to handle everything on your plate right now. It's a busy time, with the Moon moving through your career sector.

11 Don't bite off more than you can chew because chewing like crazy to get it all done will give you a sore face. Once again, you should be looking at prioritising your workload.

12 There may be issues with younger members of your family, but maybe you've spread yourself so thinly that you don't quite know who you should give your remaining time to. As with yesterday's advice, prioritise.

13 Sometimes, trying to tell others what to do, even though you know that it's the best way, will only incite their anger. Your persuasive skills will be tested today.

14 You could find yourself up against a group of people who are rather obscene, and when responding to them in the most appropriate way, you still find it difficult to cope. You do realise you don't have to spend time with them, right?

15 There may be problems with your skin or some other allergic reaction that requires a quick visit to the chemist just now. Check your diet, and keep a diary of things that may be triggering these allergies.

16 Someone is sponging off you—not necessarily financially, but in terms of your time and energy. You feel guilty saying no to them. But remember that it's your choice.

17 The new Moon indicates a developing interest in psychological subjects and self-help books to improve your mind. This is not only about understanding yourself, but about gaining a greater insight into others.

18 There's nothing worse than having to declare your credibility, if it's in question. It will sound like you're exaggerating your good points and bragging. You should let your actions speak louder than words just now.

19 Today, it's going to be difficult to find a resolution to a relationship squabble if your inner self is out of sync with your actions. Consistency is your key word.

20 There are no laws to romance as such, but if you look back at the frightening history of relationships, you might feel today that there should be. You could always create your own.

21 Your image is getting stronger just now, and you'll feel as if a new you is emerging. This may have an important impact on your finances, too. Make sure it's the best image you can project.

22 You need to get out and about, put on some new clothes, and really spruce yourself up. You've got itchy feet and are ready to go.

23 If you foresee that the sequel to a social situation is not going to be pleasant, you may be prepared to disguise yourself before going out today. What about not going out at all?

24 You can finally decide on a course of action regarding a matter around the home today. You want to implement the proper changes, but so far haven't had the will to do so. Now it's a different matter.

25 You could automatically sock it to someone today if some of their off-hand statements are too much to take. Instant retaliation—the classic bomb—may be a little heavy-handed, though.

26 Relationship issues that are emerging may need to be dealt with through approaching a friend who can act as a mentor. The older and wiser they are, the more interesting their spin on things will be. Listen carefully.

27 A bit of rock 'n' roll, alcohol and good old-fashioned fun is called for at an occasion to which you're invited. If the crowd is a little young, however, you could feel out of sorts.

28 You don't need to be fake if you're trying to improve yourself at the moment. Keep it real and, of course, dress to your age and social class. This is all the more important if you're trying to make a great first impression.

29 There could be a few days just now where the Moon ushers in a lack of energy. Either rest your body, or increase your intake of vitamins and minerals.

30 If you're feeling vulnerable today, you won't want to spend time with others, even if the invitation is enticing. Wait until you regain some of your personal strength.

31 Your statements could be confused because you yourself are confused about the topic. Brush up on the information and get some clarity before you try to explain this to others.

SEPTEMBER

 Monthly Highlight

This is another expensive month, and your taste for luxury could exceed your ability to pay for it. Try to be more practical with your finances, and resist spending money you don't have.

An opportunity to reconnect with family after the 18th means there's a welcome relief from your normal day-to-day grind.

1 You and your partner have different agendas that are pulling you in different directions, and this could confuse you today. Try to accommodate their point of view.

2 It is worthwhile getting in tune with the one you love so that your physical intimacy is in sync. This is the way to build on other aspects of your relationship as well.

3 A sudden turnaround in a partnership could leave your reeling. You assumed someone's word was good enough, but that may prove not to be the case.

4   Don't fall prey to feeling victimised just now. Take full responsibility for your decisions and their outcomes. Pointing the finger won't get you out of your dilemma.

5   You may have overlooked booking a ticket or grabbing a special deal that was on offer, and realise now that you've missed out. You may kick yourself, but don't forget that specials come up regularly— there'll be another chance.

6   People appear to be needy right now, but don't overlook the fact they're simply not pulling their own weight. Why help someone when they are not prepared to help themselves?

7   You can be decisive, persuasive and make demands without being too hard. Kill others with kindness to get them to do your bidding.

8   There is a hint of romance in your workplace just now, but you may not be able to act upon it. This could be making it a little more exciting, too.

9   The continuing transit of Venus in the area of your friendships makes life sweet at the moment. Friends are genuinely caring and a comfort to be around. Make the most of them.

10 If success has eluded you, it could be because you are in the habit of *not being successful*. One of the best kept karmic secrets is to act as if you are bringing the universe into harmony with your ambitions. By experiencing the feeling of wealth, you will attract it.

11 Your profits are definitely up, and you can look forward to an increase in income—particularly your salary—and it's been a while coming. Don't forget to ask for better working conditions while you are at it.

12 It is not a great time for teamwork just now, and you prefer to be doing things on your own. If you can get away from the office with your work in tow, you will get so much more done.

13 Today's a contrast to yesterday. Now that you have planned your work, the old adage 'many hands make light work' is the perfect summary of how you will get more done today.

14 You could be receiving some extra special treatment from others today, and you will be wondering why. No need to question it; just enjoy it, Virgo.

15 Things are changing right now, including your attitude towards others. This could be causing some problems in their dealings with you, but you've got the leverage, so keep going with what works.

16 It's a new Moon now, which indicates that your financial circumstances are ready for an overhaul. You have a shot at a bigger and better opportunity. Don't turn it down.

17 Success is not for the faint of heart. You have to try something that may involve a little fear. Trust the universe as long as your intentions are pure.

18 Make sure your heart is in the job, because that will add the finishing touch to your work. It will captivate the attention of someone who matters just now.

19 Your gut feeling may be spot on regarding a disagreement, but if you raise the issue now, it may cause an intense argument. Let it slide and wait for a more appropriate moment.

20 Your intuition is strong today, so read between the lines—your intuitive responses to people will be correct. Someone may be trying to mislead you.

21 Consider pooling your resources with a family member to purchase property if you don't have enough money to do so on your own. Real estate is high on your agenda today.

22 This is an exciting day for you, with the opportunity to create something out of nothing. You will be surprised at what's waiting for you if only you look for it.

23 Someone of romantic interest may seem so far away, but that's all in your imagination. Your mobile phone has their number in it. Call them.

24 You need to extend your creative love to every aspect of your life just now. This will bring happiness to everything you do, not just your hobbies or extra-curricular interests.

25 There are dramas in your work at present, and you may be over it all. If possible, it's best to stay out of the crossfire in any workplace disagreement.

26 You should now act on any great new ideas you have, as outlandish as they sound. You will have the co-operation of others, even if their initial reaction is a little sceptical.

27 Ideas continue to be the focus for you today, but there may be some sort of creative block obstructing the expression of these magnificent concepts. Surrender to the flow of life.

28 If you have been contemplating a new life direction, then it is likely you will want to make the change very shortly. Make sure you've tied up all the loose ends first.

29 Don't jump the gun when it comes to investing money or purchasing something a little out of your price range. You can probably get the item cheaper in the store next door. Check it out.

30 It is a full Moon, and although you realise that the success of your endeavours takes time, you may feel tired from all your careful planning not gaining any results. This is understandable, but curb your impulses anyway.

❧ OCTOBER ❧

Monthly Highlight

Venus and the Sun make you feel excited about relationships and your general social activities this month. This is a self-beautifying period where you can pamper yourself and do something you have wanted to do for a long time (but were perhaps constrained from doing so).

After the 25th, you may hear news of an increase in pay, or some lost money may resurface.

1 Allow your dreams to get bigger and bigger every day. You may be feeling that something you're wishing for may be impossible, but it isn't. Plan your life, and then live your plan.

2 One of your parents may be having troubles with which you can't help. Compassion, in this case, simply means listening attentively.

3 It's the sundry items in your life that you're probably struggling with just now. You may think that a small job here and there isn't going to impact on your primary activities, but they will. Illuminate the unnecessary.

4 You may be casting judgements on people or entering into head-on confrontations unnecessarily, all because you need to get information on a subject first-hand. Study, study, study.

5 You can't leave your current place of employment or work situation without having an adequately enticing profile. It's time, once again, to brush up your résumé.

6 Things should improve after a tumultuous start with someone new at work. Try to withhold complaints until you give them a chance to accustom themselves to the position.

7 Love should blossom under this transit, with the Moon influencing your marital affairs and friendships in a positive way. It's an enjoyable time.

8 A social occasion may be temporarily interrupted by a bolt from the blue. You'll need to re-engage with those people at a later date.

9 The insensitivity of someone may start to seem like a long winding detour from the road of friendship. You need to pull away and reappraise the situation.

10 Shopping and dealing with others will be irritating today. It could make you feel as if you don't want to have anything to do with anyone. As soon as you are finished, shut down.

11 Don't assume too much of a superior position today or you may be cut down to size. Exhibit some humility.

12 Make your presence one of commitment and involvement with the people with whom you're presently in contact. Half-hearted efforts on your part will be easily noticed by others.

13 The tack you're taking to improve a relationship may backfire. It could be costly, and you should predict the outcome by carefully studying the other person's reactions in the past.

14 You'll be busily engaged in renegotiating workplace agreements or trying to get a straight answer from an employer today.

15 It's a new Moon, and this year it seems like money is going to be an important point of contention at times. Others are being slack financially, and you need to remind them of this to cut back on expenses.

16 Today's not a day for doing more than you can handle. It's all about taking up the issue and finding a happy medium.

17 You need to renegotiate the terms of an agreement, but may be fearful that it's an all-or-nothing situation. However, this is in your imagination.

18 Today is a day for deepening your interest in friendships, but you should also include your family in your plans. There's a crossover between your family and your social life.

19 You need to make an extra effort with someone in the family, possibly a child who's not behaving properly. Try not to react too strongly, and say it with a smile.

20 Why not be a little bit frivolous, because the day calls for some fun and the offloading of serious topics. You can enjoy the company of others with a few jokes.

21 A lover may be concealing their intentions, but this is not for any malicious reason. Try to see the bigger picture with them.

22 If you've got something to say, even if it's a little weird, it will have the desired effect—that is, gaining the attention of someone.

23 Being different continues to be the theme for you to attract attention. You need to step outside your normal way of seeing and doing things, and explore the possibilities.

24 Don't let others be the judge of your relationships. It's time to take your most personal relationship away from prying eyes.

25 It's important to eliminate distractions during this two-day cycle. If you're trying to get to know someone more deeply, this should simply be in a one-on-one format.

26 You need to restart a business relationship, even though you're reluctant to do so. You may have to assume a dominant posture at this time.

27 Create a more intimate rapport with a client or business associate by writing an e-mail or telephoning them. You need to get closer to this person to reap the financial benefits.

28 You mustn't look at the pot of gold at the end of the rainbow, but at the practicalities of what's involved in a business deal. Admittedly, the end goal does seem dazzlingly attractive.

29 It's sad, but sometimes others have to point out certain attributes in us before we can improve ourselves. Take the criticism on the chin and continue to grow.

30 You need a discussion about your responsibilities and those of your partner, so that you can gain a clearer understanding of what's what, and who's who. This will make things better.

31 The growing distance between you and your lover has to do with additional responsibilities and work today. Give them assurances that the situation is not permanent.

❦ NOVEMBER ❧

Monthly Highlight

Relationships are on the up and up, and a new romance could appear out of nowhere after the 11th.

If you are a parent, conflicts with children can be avoided, but only if you dedicate a lot more time to the cause. Try to connect with your inner child during this month.

1 You're quick off the mark with your speech, but may antagonise someone with the words you use. It is essential to choose your words more carefully just now.

2 You may reluctantly need to go with the flow, particularly if you're opposed to a course of action being taken by your peer group. Don't resist the plan until you get a taste of it.

3 A hazy assessment of someone at the outset could present problems for you down the track. Don't be lazy in studying people a little more carefully just now.

4   Your determination is powerful at present. Even if you're unclear as to the outcomes of your actions, your drive for success will bring you the desired results.

5   If you're feeling imprisoned by a certain situation today, don't continue to turn your mind away from the problem. Take the bull by the horns and quickly come up with a solution.

6   You may have some sort of epiphany today, a realisation that your hard work and dedication hasn't been wasted or taken for granted. This is a time of renewed confidence.

7   You feel a rather large gap between where you are and what used to be moments of great pleasure and self-satisfaction. Try to recapture some of the feeling in what you do.

8   You're robust in serving others and relentless in pleasing them, but now it's time for them to give back to you. Demand that your rights are met and fulfilled.

9   Stop relying on your addictive patterns of rational deduction. Feel with your heart if you want to come up with the right answer today.

10 The only way you're going to reassure yourself about financial matters is to address the problem of receipts, statements and other practical issues you've previously avoided. Get cracking!

11 It would be a shame to rely on other people to measure your self-worth. You don't need their approval. Trust your own judgement today.

12 You're impressive today, ferreting out a problem in your dealings with a service technician such as a mechanic or other handyman. Don't let them pull the wool over your eyes.

13 The new Moon prompts you to investigate educational work programs that will further develop your skills. If you've been bored, this is an excellent time to stimulate your mind.

14 Mercury and Mars have made you angry, and you're levelling these emotions at the people you love most. You're hurting yourself, and you don't even know it.

15 If you stand up for a companion, you may end up getting burnt. Don't be an ethical or moral cover for someone who should be taking responsibility for their own actions.

16 Someone's rushing you—it's not that you don't agree, but you need gradual change just now. Explain your position to them.

17 You could be confined in your location, but there's a simple solution to this—get out! It's a day in which the sun, air, earth and sea are your saviours.

18 An inbuilt redundancy can make you feel angry today, especially if a device or piece of electronic equipment is fairly new and it fails. Being frustrated won't help you pay for a new one, though, will it?

19 You may realise you've fallen foul of someone who's subsequently snagged you in an agreement or contract. There may be no way out of this except to chalk it up to experience.

20 All you need now is a pure, friendly and simple companion to get you through this current cycle. Fortunately, your magnetic appeal has brought you exactly that. This should be a positive day.

21 You'll be in the hot seat today if you've been chosen to instruct others and you don't know your stuff. Being forewarned is being forearmed.

22 Don't take your powers for granted just now. Strength means knowing how to restrain yourself as well. This way you have control, but you also maintain respect.

23 A pseudo-copyright is not sufficient today. You need to protect your ideas, sketches and any other business concepts you have. Don't hold back on an expense if it can protect you.

24 Your mind may be congested by information overload. You have to strip things back to basics—this will be your reality check today.

25 Things from the past, like antiques, may interest you today, especially if you're thinking of exploring interior design or other home-based activities. It's a creative day.

26 You have to be systematic and strategic in your work just now. This relates to meeting deadlines, but also to handling some pretty tricky characters.

27 A corrupt benefit leaves you open to damage in future. If you can't deal with someone's enticements face to face, put up the unavailable sign.

28 It's the full Moon and, once again, you may be emotional. At work, don't derive your conclusions from what may be misleading information. Check your facts.

29 You're forced to use equipment that may not be to your liking today. You can either resist this forever or try to learn a new methodology.

30 You could hear some news that inspires or transforms you just now. This will also serve to make you work harder to achieve your ambition.

❧ DECEMBER ❧

 Monthly Highlight

This last month of 2012 should be rather creative, but you may have divided loyalties over whether to give yourself some time or finish off important work at the office.

Mars is in the sixth zone of health and work colleagues, so be careful not to work yourself up over a dispute with a co-worker.

1 You've got a new lease on life today when it comes to friendships, and you won't be waiting around for anyone who's dragging their feet. It's off into the car and out into the nightlife for you, Virgo.

2 Don't let the little things make you obsessive just now. Something like a casual remark may have you stewing, when, in fact, nothing was meant by it.

3   A situation may have a few different sides to it, and make you feel very aware of your shortcomings and the need for a different approach. Don't underestimate your own power, though.

4   The gap between you and another person is growing, but what are you going to do about it? If a heart-to-heart talk doesn't work, you may doubt the value of this person.

5   Your diplomatic skills could be called upon to resolve a situation between two friends. Try to remain impartial to what you hear.

6   If too much work is falling on your shoulders and others aren't sharing the load, you'll have words with them today, and so you should.

7   You might be experiencing a creative block just now. Even though you have many ideas, the words and actions simply aren't flowing. Put your thoughts aside until you feel creatively stimulated again.

8   Your boss may be a stick in the mud and unable to see your reasoning for a course of action, no matter how much you explain it. You may have to let it go.

9 Once again, you're finding you have to prove your worth, because you're only as good as your last hit, as they say in the music business. You need tangible results to prove yourself.

10 Your instincts are sharp, and you have the ability to sniff out a deal, particularly in sales or marketing. Go where the money is just now.

11 You can be successful without offending others, even if they are being obnoxious. Use your friends and allies, and don't lower your standards.

12 You need to step outside your normal approach to love and romance to explore other possibilities. This will be hard for your partner, but they'll get used to it soon enough.

13 You're finally starting to see that there is a different way to deal with your family relationships. Practice makes perfect, and today you'll see some positive results.

14 Try to be objective about a current romantic scenario. Give the other person a chance to steer it their way for a while, and see where you end up.

15 If you're feeling stagnant, it's time to get out and about. Sign up at your local gym. You're feeling lazy, and need to do something to counter it.

16 If you're piqued by a neighbour or someone in your workplace who has an annoying habit, you may need to find other ways to block them out, because talking won't work.

17 It's reconciliation time, and if something about a friend is bothering you, you need to discuss the issues. They may be a little scared they're losing you, but you can resolve things together.

18 You may be accused of holding out on others because you're not prepared to share your ideas too quickly. Let them think what they want—they're your ideas, after all.

19 Being open and transparent with someone just now creates the risk of a disagreement, but that's a sacrifice you're willing to make to get to the truth.

20 Misunderstandings will continue today unless you put on your listening ears. Pay special attention to what's being said, and try your hardest to be conciliatory.

21 If you've decided to hear an expert speak or get a professional opinion and you don't agree with it, you'll be anything but fulfilled, especially if you've paid money. But sometimes we just have to grin and bear the fact that worthless advice has a cost.

22 You have to put a positive spin on a situation today, even if the day starts off on a bad note. Try to see what happens more as an opportunity rather than an obstacle.

23 It might be like trying to relax on a razorblade today with all the work you have to finish. Take things in your stride, and don't get angry over trifling matters.

24 Merry Christmas, Virgo! Unfortunately, work will be on your mind, and you may not be able to relax enough to enjoy the festivities. But it is a holiday, after all, so forget work.

25 Use a low-key manner in dealing with everyone from the local shopkeeper to family members today. This method will get you the best results, and you may make a new friend or two as well.

26 You mustn't let an incompatibility of philosophies ruin a possible breakthrough in your intimacy with someone. Put aside your personal beliefs, and accept each other for who you are.

27 You could meet a new friend who's prepared to give you and your friendship a good try. It could be someone you've overlooked in the past.

28 You might find yourself in possession of some free extras for your office or home. There's no catch, just a matter of being in the right place at the right time.

29 You'll be feeling abstract today. Unless you can connect with someone who is also eclectic and interested in mentally travelling to unusual places with you, it's best to keep to yourself.

30 You may have to deal with a group of older people, even if it feels uncomfortable. There may be some unusual lessons in these last days of the year for you, Virgo.

31 It's all systems go as you now decide to implement some of your plans and strategies. As the new year dawns you feel confident that you can tackle any coming challenges with confidence. You will finish the year on a high.

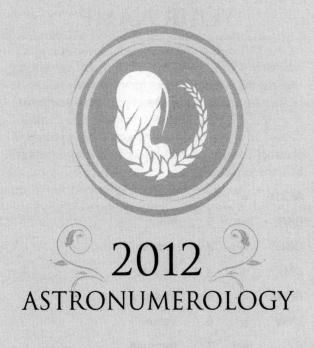

2012
ASTRONUMEROLOGY

THE BEST WAY TO PREPARE FOR LIFE
IS TO BEGIN TO LIVE.

Elbert Hubbard

THE POWER BEHIND YOUR NAME

It's hard to believe that your name resonates with a numerical vibration, but it's true! Simply by adding together the numbers of your name, you can see which planet rules you and what effects your name will have on your life and destiny. According to the ancient Chaldean system of numerology, each number is assigned a planetary energy, and each alphabetical letter a number, as in the following list:

AIQJY	=	1	Sun
BKR	=	2	Moon
CGLS	=	3	Jupiter
DMT	=	4	Uranus
EHNX	=	5	Mercury
UVW	=	6	Venus
OZ	=	7	Neptune
FP	=	8	Saturn
—	=	9	Mars

Note: The number 9 is not allotted a letter because it was considered 'unknowable'.

Once the numbers have been added, you can establish which single planet rules your name and personal affairs. At this point the number 9 can be used for interpretation. Do you think it's unusual that many famous actors, writers and musicians modify their names? This is to attract luck and good fortune, which can be made easier by using the energies of a friendlier planet. Try experimenting with the table and see how new names affect you. It's so much fun, and you may even attract greater love, wealth and worldly success!

Look at the following example to work out the power of your name. A person named Andrew Brown would calculate his ruling planet by correlating each letter to a number in the table, like this:

A	N	D	R	E	W		B	R	O	W	N
1	5	4	2	5	6		2	2	7	6	5

And then add the numbers like this:

$1 + 5 + 4 + 2 + 5 + 6 + 2 + 2 + 7 + 6 + 5$ = 45

Then add $4 + 5$ = 9

The ruling number of Andrew Brown's name is 9, which is governed by Mars (see how the 9 can now be used?). Now study the Name-Number Table to reveal the power of your name. The numbers 4 and 5 will play a secondary role in Andrew's character and destiny, so in his case you would also study the effects of Uranus (4) and Mercury (5).

Name Number	Ruling Planet	Name Characteristics
1	Sun	Attractive personality. Magnetic charm. Superman- or superwoman-like vitality and physical energy. Incredibly active and gregarious. Enjoys outdoor activities and sports. Has friends in powerful positions. Good government connections. Intelligent, spectacular, flashy and successful. A loyal number for love and relationships.
2	Moon	Feminine and soft, with an emotional temperament. Fluctuating moods but intuitive, possibly even has clairvoyant abilities. Ingenious nature. Expresses feelings kind-heartedly. Loves family, motherhood and home life. Night owl who probably needs more sleep. Success with the public and/or women generally.

Name Number	Ruling Planet	Name Characteristics
3	Jupiter	A sociable, optimistic number with a fortunate destiny. Attracts opportunities without too much effort. Great sense of timing. Religious or spiritual inclinations. Naturally drawn to investigating the meaning of life. Philosophical insight. Enjoys travel, explores the world and different cultures.
4	Uranus	Volatile character with many peculiar aspects. Likes to experiment and test novel experiences. Forward-thinking, with many extraordinary friends. Gets bored easily so needs plenty of inspiring activities. Pioneering, technological and creative. Wilful and obstinate at times. Unforeseen events in life may be positive or negative.

Name Number	Ruling Planet	Name Characteristics
5	Mercury	Sharp-witted and quick-thinking, with great powers of speech. Extremely active in life: always on the go and living on nervous energy. Has a youthful outlook and never grows old— looks younger than actual age. Has young friends and a humorous disposition. Loves reading and writing. Great communicator.
6	Venus	Delightful and charming personality. Graceful and eye-catching. Cherishes and nourishes friends. Very active social life. Musical or creative interests. Has great money-making opportunities as well as numerous love affairs. A career in the public eye is quite likely. Loves family, but often troubled over divided loyalties with friends.

Name Number	Ruling Planet	Name Characteristics
7	Neptune	Intuitive, spiritual and self-sacrificing nature. Easily duped by those who need help. Loves to dream of life's possibilities. Has healing powers. Dreams are revealing and prophetic. Loves the water and will have many journeys in life. Spiritual aspirations dominate worldly desires.
8	Saturn	Hard-working, ambitious person with slow yet certain achievements. Remarkable concentration and self-sacrifice for a chosen objective. Financially focused, but generous when a person's trust is gained. Proficient in his or her chosen field but a hard taskmaster. Demands perfection and needs to relax and enjoy life more.

Name Number	Ruling Planet	Name Characteristics
9	Mars	Extraordinary physical drive, desires and ambition. Sports and outdoor activities are major keys to health. Confrontational, but likes to work and play really hard. Protects and defends family, friends and territory. Has individual tastes in life, but is also self-absorbed. Needs to listen to others' advice to gain greater success.

YOUR PLANETARY
RULER

Astrology and numerology are intimately connected. Each planet rules over a number between 1 and 9. Both your name and your birth date are governed by planetary energies. As described earlier, here are the planets and their ruling numbers:

1   **Sun**

2   **Moon**

3   **Jupiter**

4   **Uranus**

5   **Mercury**

6   **Venus**

7   **Neptune**

8   **Saturn**

9   **Mars**

To find out which planet will control the coming year for you, simply add the numbers of your birth date and the year in question. An example follows.

If you were born on 14 November, add the numerals 1 and 4 (14, your day of birth) and 1 and 1 (11, your month of birth) to the year in question, in this case 2012 (current year), like this:

Add 1 + 4 + 1 + 1 + 2 + 0 + 1 + 2   = 12

1 + 2   = 3

Thus, the planet ruling your individual karma for 2012 would be Jupiter, because this planet rules the number 3.

YOUR PLANETARY FORECAST

You can even take your ruling name number, as discussed previously, and add it to the year in question to throw more light on your coming personal affairs, like this:

A N D R E W B R O W N   =   9

Year coming   =   2012

Add 9 + 2 + 0 + 1 + 2   =   14

Add 1 + 4   =   5

Thus, this would be the ruling year number based on your name number. Therefore, you would study the influence of Mercury (5) using the Trends for Your Planetary Number table in 2012. Enjoy!

Trends for Your Planetary Number in 2012

Year Number	Ruling Planet	Results Throughout the Coming Year
1	Sun	**Overview**

Overview

The commencement of a new cycle: a year full of accomplishments, increased reputation and brand new plans and projects.

Many new responsibilities. Success and strong physical vitality. Health should improve and illnesses will be healed.

If you have ailments, now is the time to improve your physical wellbeing—recovery will be certain.

Love and pleasure

A lucky year for love. Creditable connections with children, family life is in focus. Music, art and creative expression will be fulfilling. New romantic opportunities.

Work

Minimal effort for maximum luck. Extra money and exciting opportunities professionally. Positive new changes result in promotion and pay rises.

Improving your luck

Luck is plentiful throughout the year, but especially in July and August. The 1st, 8th, 15th and 22nd hours of Sundays are lucky.

Lucky numbers are 1, 10, 19 and 28.

Year Number	Ruling Planet	Results Throughout the Coming Year
2	Moon	**Overview**

Overview

Reconnection with your emotions and past. Excellent for relationships with family members. Moodiness may become a problem. Sleeping patterns will be affected.

Love and pleasure

Home, family life and relationships are focused in 2012. Relationships improve through self-effort and greater communication. Residential changes, renovations and interior decoration bring satisfaction. Increased psychic sensitivity.

Work

Emotional in work. Home career, or hobby from a domestic base, will bring greater income opportunities. Females will be more prominent in your work.

Improving your luck

July will fulfil some of your dreams. Mondays will be lucky: the 1st, 8th, 15th and 22nd hours of them are the most fortunate. Pay special attention to the new and full Moons in 2012.

Lucky numbers include 2, 11, 20, 29 and 38.

Year Number	Ruling Planet	Results Throughout the Coming Year
3	Jupiter	**Overview**

Overview

A lucky year for you. Exciting opportunities arise to expand horizons. Good fortune financially. Travels and increased popularity. A happy year. Spiritual, humanitarian and self-sacrificial focus. Self-improvement is likely.

Love and pleasure

Speculative in love. May meet someone new to travel with, or travel with your friends and lovers. Gambling results in some wins and some losses. Current relationships will deepen in their closeness.

Work

Fortunate for new opportunities and success. Employers are more accommodating and open to your creative expression. Extra money. Promotions are quite possible.

Improving your luck

Remain realistic, get more sleep and don't expect too much from your efforts. Planning is necessary for better luck. The 1st, 8th, 15th and 24th hours of Thursdays are spiritually very lucky for you.

Lucky numbers this year are 3, 12, 21 and 30. March and December are lucky months. The year 2012 will bring some unexpected surprises.

Year Number	Ruling Planet	Results Throughout the Coming Year
4	Uranus	**Overview**

Overview

Unexpected events, both pleasant and sometimes unpleasant, are likely. Difficult choices appear. Break free of your past and self-imposed limitations. An independent year in which a new path will be forged. Discipline is necessary. Structure your life appropriately, even if doing so is difficult.

Love and pleasure

Guard against dissatisfaction in relationships. Need freedom and experimentation. May meet someone out of the ordinary. Emotional and sexual explorations. Spirituality and community service enhanced. Many new friendships.

Work

Progress is made in work. Technology and other computer or Internet-related industries are fulfilling. Increased knowledge and work skills. New opportunities arise when they are least expected. Excessive work and tension. Learn to relax. Efficiency in time essential. Work with groups and utilise networks to enhance professional prospects.

Year Number	Ruling Planet	Results Throughout the Coming Year
		Improving your luck

Moderation is the key word. Be patient and do not rush things. Slow your pace this year, as being impulsive will only lead to errors and missed opportunities. Exercise greater patience in all matters. Steady investments are lucky.

The 1st, 8th, 15th and 20th hours of any Saturday will be very lucky in 2012.

Your lucky numbers are 4, 13, 22 and 31.

Year Number	Ruling Planet	Results Throughout the Coming Year
5	Mercury	

Overview

Intellectual activities and communication increases. Imagination is powerful. Novel and exciting new concepts will bring success and personal satisfaction.

Goal-setting will be difficult. Acquire the correct information before making decisions. Develop concentration and stay away from distracting or negative people.

Love and pleasure

Give as much as you take in relationships. Changes in routine are necessary to keep your love life upbeat and progressive. Develop open-mindedness.

Avoid being critical of your partner. Keep your opinions to yourself. Artistic pursuits and self-improvement are factors in your relationships.

Work

Become a leader in your field in 2012. Contracts, new job offers and other agreements open up new pathways to success. Develop business skills.

Speed, efficiency and capability are your key words this year. Don't be impulsive in making any career changes. Travel is also on the agenda.

Year Number	Ruling Planet	Results Throughout the Coming Year

Improving your luck

Write ideas down, research topics more thoroughly, communicate enthusiasm through meetings—this will afford you much more luck. Stick to one idea.

The 1st, 8th, 15th and 20th hours of Wednesdays are luckiest, so schedule meetings and other important social engagements at these times.

Throughout 2012 your lucky numbers are 5, 14, 23 and 32.

Year Number	Ruling Planet	Results Throughout the Coming Year
6	Venus	

Overview

A year of love. Expect romantic and sensual interludes, and new love affairs. Number 6 is also related to family life. Working with a loved one or family member is possible, with good results. Save money, cut costs. Share success.

Love and pleasure

The key word for 2012 is romance. Current relationships are deepened. New relationships will be formed and may have some karmic significance, especially if single. Spend time grooming and beautifying yourself: put your best foot forward. Engagement and even marriage is possible. Increased social responsibilities. Moderate excessive tendencies.

Work

Further interest in financial matters and future material security. Reduce costs and become frugal. Extra cash is likely. Additional income or bonuses are possible. Working from home may also be of interest. Social activities and work coincide.

Year Number	Ruling Planet	Results Throughout the Coming Year
		Improving your luck

Work and success depend on a creative and positive mental attitude. Eliminate bad habits and personal tendencies that are obstructive. Balance spiritual and financial needs.

The 1st, 8th, 15th and 20th hours on Fridays are extremely lucky this year, and new opportunities can arise when they are least expected.

The numbers 6, 15, 24 and 33 will generally increase your luck.

Year Number	Ruling Planet	Results Throughout the Coming Year
7	Neptune	

Overview

An intuitive and spiritual year. Your life path becomes clear. Focus on your inner powers to gain a greater understanding and perspective of your true mission in life. Remove emotional baggage. Make peace with past lovers who have hurt or betrayed you. Forgiveness is the key word this year.

Love and pleasure

Spend time loving yourself, not just bending over backwards for others. Sacrifice to those who are worthy. Relationships should be reciprocal. Avoid deception, swindling or other forms of gossip. Affirm what you want in a relationship to your lover. Set high standards.

Work

Unselfish work is the key to success. Learn to say no to demanding employers or co-workers. Remove clutter to make space for bigger and better things. Healing and caring professions may feature strongly. Use your intuition to manoeuvre carefully into new professional directions.

Year Number	Ruling Planet	Results Throughout the Coming Year

Improving your luck

Maintain cohesive lines of communication and stick to one path for best results. Pay attention to health and don't let stress affect a positive outlook. Sleep well, exercise and develop better eating habits to improve energy circulation.

The 1st, 8th, 15th and 20th hours of Wednesdays are luckiest, so schedule meetings and other important social engagements at these times.

Throughout 2012 your lucky numbers are 7, 16, 25 and 34.

Year Number	Ruling Planet	Results Throughout the Coming Year
8	Saturn	

Overview

This is a practical year requiring effort, hard work and a certain amount of solitude for best results. Pay attention to structure, timelines and your diary. Don't try to help too many people, but rather, focus on yourself. This will be a year of discipline and self-analysis. However, income levels will eventually increase.

Love and pleasure

Balance personal affairs with work. Show affection to loved ones through practicality and responsibility.

Dedicate time to family, not just work. Schedule activities outdoors for increased wellbeing and emotional satisfaction.

Work

Money is on the increase this year, but continued focus is necessary. Hard work equals extra income. A cautious and resourceful year, but be generous where possible. Some new responsibilities will bring success. Balance income potential with creative satisfaction.

Year Number	Ruling Planet	Results Throughout the Coming Year

Improving your luck

Being overcautious and reluctant to attempt something new will cause delay and frustration if new opportunities are offered. Be kind to yourself and don't overwork or overdo exercise. Send out positive thought-waves to friends and loved ones. The karmic energy will return.

The 1st, 8th, 15th and 20th hours of Saturdays are the best times for you in 2012.

The numbers 1, 8, 17, 26 and 35 are lucky.

Year Number	Ruling Planet	Results Throughout the Coming Year
9	Mars	

Overview

The ending of one chapter of your life and the preparation for the beginning of a new cycle. A transition period when things may be in turmoil or a state of uncertainty. Remain calm. Do not be impulsive or irritable. Avoid arguments. Calm communication will help find solutions.

Love and pleasure

Tremendous energy and drive help you achieve goals this year. But don't be too pushy when forcing your ideas down other people's throats, so to speak. Diplomatic discussions, rather than arguments, should be used to achieve outcomes. Discuss changes before making decisions with partners and lovers in your life.

Work

A successful year with the expectation of bigger and better things next year. Driven by work objectives or ambition. Tendency to overdo and overwork. Pace your deadlines. Leadership role likely. Respect and honour from your peers and employers.

Year Number	Ruling Planet	Results Throughout the Coming Year
		Improving your luck
		Find adequate outlets for your high level of energy through meditation, self-reflection and prayer. Collect your energies and focus them on one point. Release tension to maintain health.
		The 1st, 8th, 15th and 20th hours of Tuesdays will be lucky for you throughout 2012.
		Your lucky numbers are 9, 18, 27 and 36.